Praise for
The Ministry of Motherhood

"*The Ministry of Motherhood* is the story of one mother who has dared to go beyond the ordinary in loving, leading, and training her children to follow Christ. In this honest and inspiring book, Sally Clarkson paints a stirring vision of a mother's mission and challenges women to disciple their children to be passionate, devoted servants of Christ."

—NANCY LEIGH DEMOSS, author and host of *Revive Our Hearts Radio*

"Biblical, practical, motivational. This inspiring book belongs on every mother's nightstand."

—LINDA DILLOW, author of *Calm My Anxious Heart* and coauthor of *Intimate Issues*

"Here we have a book to substantiate that the ministry of motherhood and the Great Commission are not mutually exclusive but a complement and catalyst to each other! With an extraordinary blend of humility, challenge, and encouragement, Sally gives an exalted vision to our calling and stewardship as mothers."

—DEBBY THOMPSON, wife and mother with thirty years of ministry leadership, currently with Campus Crusade for ͨ ͤͬn Europe and Russia

"If you feel like a hamster on a wʰ   getting anywhere—then *The Minis.*   ͧy Clarkson inspires us to step off that wheel a   ͭͤse, not by adding something else to our hectic schedu   ͬinging God into everything we do. With down-to-earth, praͨ ͽal examples, she shows us how we, too, can build disciples as we reach our children's hearts. A very encouraging and easy-to-read book!"

—SHEILA WRAY GREGOIRE, author of *To Love, Honor, and Vacuum*

"My thanks to Sally Clarkson for her sacrifice and dedication and the example her life has been to me. Through her writings she is able to share some of what God has put on her heart. This book, along with her others, reveals her to be a shining example of one committed to honor God in all she does. May you be blessed as you read this book and continue this journey we call motherhood."

—LYNN VANWINGERDEN, wife, mother of twenty-three children, grandmother of nine

Praise for
The Mission of Motherhood

"Sally Clarkson has achieved a beautiful balance of biblical teaching and the heart of a mother in *The Mission of Motherhood*. She gently takes the reader by the hand and stands with her before the truth of her calling. Readers will be entertained by her personal stories, empowered by God's call to mothers, and encouraged by Sally's teaching."

—VICKI CARUANA, author of the best-selling *Apples & Chalkdust* and founder of EncourageTeachers.com

"In *The Mission of Motherhood*, Sally Clarkson invites the reader into her family and into her heart to see 'mother' in action: teaching, comforting, training, enriching, and blessing. This book elevates the mission of motherhood and sends the reader back to her children 'pumped.' "

—JEAN FLEMING, author of *A Mother's Heart*

THE

Ministry of Motherhood

THE

The Ministry of Motherhood

FOLLOWING CHRIST'S EXAMPLE IN REACHING

THE HEARTS *of* OUR CHILDREN

SALLY CLARKSON

WATERBROOK

THE MINISTRY OF MOTHERHOOD

All Scripture quotations, unless otherwise indicated, are taken from the New American Standard Bible®. © Copyright The Lockman Foundation 1960, 1962, 1963, 1968, 1971, 1972, 1973, 1975, 1977, 1995. Used by permission. (www.Lockman.org). Scripture quotations marked (NKJV) are taken from the New King James Version. Copyright © 1982 by Thomas Nelson, Inc. Used by permission. All rights reserved.

Trade Paperback ISBN 978-1-57856-582-5
eBook ISBN 978-0-307-56410-8

Copyright © 2004 by Sally Clarkson

Published in the United States by WaterBrook, an imprint of the Crown Publishing Group, a division of Penguin Random House LLC, New York.

WATERBROOK® and its deer colophon are registered trademarks of Penguin Random House LLC.

Library of Congress Cataloging-in-Publication Data
Clarkson, Sally.
   The ministry of motherhood : following Christ's example in reaching the hearts of our children / Sally Clarkson.— 1st ed.
      p. cm.
   ISBN 1-57856-582-0
   1. Motherhood—Religious aspects—Christianity. 2. Christian education—Home training. 3. Jesus Christ—Example. I. Title.
   BV4529.18.C525 2004
   248.8'431—dc22

                                                         2003017380

Printed in the United States of America
2018

30 29 28 27 26 25 24 23 22

To my oldest child and first daughter,
Sarah,
my treasured friend.
Thank you for your ministry to the whole family
while I wrote this book.

And to my other precious children,
Joel, Nathan, and Joy.
All of you have been the focus of my ministry
the past twenty years.
May God give wind to your wings and
fulfill your deepest dreams.

CONTENTS

Discovering the Ministry of Motherhood

The small flame of the vanilla candle flickered wildly as air from the opening door fanned the flame. Sarah, my gentle oldest child, peeked in the door and asked if we could talk for a few minutes. Her quiet voice told me she didn't want to attract the attention of anyone else in the house who might want to join us.

I had come to my bedroom to be alone. A fire was lit in the fireplace, a cup of tea steamed at my side, and a gentle Celtic melody played in the background—the perfect setting for the short, one-woman retreat I had planned as a break from the otherwise busy hours of my day. Spending time with Sarah, though, was almost always a balm to my soul.

Somehow, in the past few years, we had passed from being just mother and daughter to becoming trusted and intimate soul mates. The strength we gained from our relationship had anchored both of us during several turbulent years. I had come to see my relationship with her as one of the real treasures and privileges of my life. And now, I could see, my almost-adult daughter really needed me. Her eyes were clouded over, and her face was marked with sadness. So I invited her in, and she quietly closed the door so we could sneak in a few private moments.

The tears began to overflow her dark blue eyes as soon as she sat down. The past year had been hard and lonely for her. She had yet to find a close friend in the new area where we had lived for two years. Several supposedly Christian young people had talked about dabbling in premarital sex, and some Christian leaders she knew and respected had caused the split-up of a church, leaving many broken relationships behind. On top of all this, our country had just experienced the terrorist attacks of September 11, and because my husband, Clay, and I were away at the time, Sarah had gone through that traumatic time without us. All these painful realities—plus the nagging question of what to do with the rest of her life—combined to trouble her mind and heart.

"Mom, I'm having such doubts in my Christian faith," she began. "So many of the believers I know seem passionless or mediocre, or they've compromised their faith by living immoral or immature lives. I would never believe in God if I had to depend on what I knew about him from many of the people we know!… And so many terrible things have been happening in the world; it's hard to make sense of it all.… And I want to live a life that's pleasing to Christ, but sometimes I just feel so different from my peers.… And sometimes I wonder if God is really there listening to my prayers at all. Does my life matter to anyone at all?"

I let her pour out her heart without judgment or criticism. Knowing her personal integrity, I was sure her thoughts and feelings came not from a rebellious heart but from an honest desire to find answers only God could give.

When she had finished talking, I assured her that God was big enough to sustain her questions and doubts and that he would make himself known to her in his time. Her spirit slowly calmed down.

"You know, Mom, my doubts haven't really driven me away from God; they're driving me closer to him. I really want to have an authentic faith. I want to know the real God who created the stars and gave us the gift of beauty and music and great thoughts. I want a God who is real and worthy of my desire for greatness and purpose. I'm not looking for religion; I want a close and true relationship worthy of my whole life commitment! I want what you and Daddy have. I feel like I'm just beginning to understand what you have been teaching me for so many years."

I realized then, as I have realized before, what my daughter really needs from my husband and me in this fallen, mixed-up world. It's the same thing that all my four children need—and that your children need as well.

They don't need sweet platitudes of faith that will momentarily placate their emotions. They need the authentic strength that comes from the true foundation of a biblical world-view and a proper understanding of the real Christ who is worthy of their worship. They need an unwavering, internal moral and spiritual compass that will help them weather today's storms and tomorrow's and will guide them for the rest of their lives. They also need to see what real faith looks like when lived day in, day out, so they will have a pattern to follow.

The process of providing such gifts to my children is what I've come to think of as the ministry of motherhood. I believe it's central to the calling of anyone God has privileged to bring children into this world.

If you are a mother, it's your ministry too.

THE PROCESS OF DISCIPLESHIP

Seeing Sarah struggle with her own questions and doubts reminded me in some ways of my own quest for the Lord when I was a young woman. What happened to me during those early years, in fact, helped me prepare to be a mother with a conscious ministry—reaching my children's hearts for the Lord. When I first became a Christian, I learned a pattern of discipleship that was modeled after Jesus' relationship with his disciples. This model later gave me confidence as a mother and showed me how I could have a spiritual impact on the lives of my own children.

Prior to that, however, I entered college in the turbulent early 1970s, when so much that was traditional and moral was being questioned. So many new "isms" were gaining momentum—feminism, moral relativism, and the flourishing of a secular humanism that held traditional Christianity in contempt—and I was swept right along with the tide. I questioned everything I had been taught.

My parents believed that each of their children should be sent out of state to college to develop a sense of independence in the world. So with a heart full of questions, a desire to find meaning in life, and a longing for romance and adventure, I left home and moved into my new college dorm. But I was soon disillusioned by the meaninglessness of the party lifestyle I encountered, where long-term or committed relationships were looked down on and "free love" was touted. I could see nothing "free" about this lifestyle at all; to me, it seemed to exact a precious price. All I could see in the lives of my friends was guilt, hurt feelings, and a sense of being used by the boys who were so willing to take advantage of them.

Meanwhile, I was taking university classes in which traditional biblical faith was debunked and atheism seemed to be the common philosophical foundation. Yet, none of these teachings touched the deeply felt needs of my own soul. I yearned for a sense of meaning in life. I longed for a real friend with whom I could share my doubts and joys without judgment or rejection. I longed for a reason to keep living and a sense that I had something significant to give back to the world.

During this time the Lord providentially brought me some friends who would radically change my life. One girl knocked on my dorm door and asked if I would take a religious survey. She naturally transitioned from the survey to talking with me about God and that it really is possible to know God personally. She invited me to meet with some of her friends who attended a Bible study together each week. And I accepted.

I'm sure I must have been a burden to those precious people, because I challenged everything they said. Yet I found they had intelligent, thought-through answers to my questions. Many books full of new ideas were passed my way, and we spent evenings discussing them into the wee hours over steaming mugs of coffee, French doughnuts, and salty chips—our typical dorm room cuisine.

It wasn't long before I committed my life wholeheartedly and enthusiastically to Christ. I joined another Bible study group where I was systematically taught Scripture. Even more significant, I became involved in a campus ministry, which meant that I was asked to pass on to others what I was learning.

I innocently asked some of the other girls in my dorm if they wanted to come to my room for small-group discussions and Bible study. Before I knew it, I was leading several Bible studies on campus. On weekends I would go to my training time, where I would learn the basics of my Christian faith. And then, during the week, I would meet with several other small groups of women and share with them what I had been learning.

How exciting it was to see that God wanted to use my life to reach others, even from the very beginning of my relationship with him! I was learning that God created very normal people like me to have a ministry—a spiritual impact in the lives of other people.

I vividly remember some of the great friendships I developed with people in the campus ministry group. We felt we were a vital part of an important movement. We had prayer nights in which we would hold up "lost" friends and professors we had met on campus. We got involved in public debates. We took our stories of how we came to faith into our dorms, our apartments, our fraternities and sororities.

The leaders of the campus ministry were actually just a bit older than we were, yet at the time they seemed far superior to us in their knowledge of life. I was paired with a young woman who led a group of us "leaders," the ones who taught small-group Bible studies all over campus. She seemed so much older and more knowledgeable than I because she had graduated from college a couple of years before and I was just a youngster sophomore!

She would invite me to her apartment and say, "Let's have a special lunch together." Once she opened a can of split-pea soup and made toast with cheese on it, lit some candles, and served me. I thought she was a gourmet cook just because I had never made split-pea soup myself and because she made me feel so special. When she talked to me, she would say, "You know, Sally, I believe that God has special plans for your life. You have such a love for people and such a great understanding of God's Word! I can't wait to see all of the awesome ways in which God is going to use you!"

Through these intimate meetings, studies, and group fellowship times, I really was captivated by the desire to see my life count for God's purposes. I developed a heart for personal ministry that grew out of the fullness of my own life and my relationships with friends who loved God and were willing to teach me and encourage me. My desire to minister was not based on any special background or degree; I was just a normal person who happened to love God deeply. Yet this experience seemed to answer all of my questions in a satisfactory way as well as meet my desire for purpose in life, intimate friendship and fellowship, and a sense of adventure and fun. It seemed to me that knowing Christ didn't just provide forgiveness of sins, but totally changed the outlook, values, and goals of any person who seriously sought to know and follow him.

When I came upon the passage of Matthew 4:18-22, where Jesus called his disciples to himself and asked them to drop their fishing nets and follow him, I felt I knew firsthand what that meant. I had been taken from my own typical life of empty college classes and parties into a living relationship with God, a life in which reaching the world for his glory was the overriding purpose of all other activities.

I read another passage that also seemed to relate to this idea of discipleship. When Jesus was praying the high priestly prayer the night before he was crucified, he seemed to talk to God about the purposes he had for his disciples. He said, "As You sent Me into the world, I also have sent them into the world" (John 17:18, NKJV).

It struck me that just as Jesus had come into the world to teach people about God, redeem them back to him, and show them his kingdom purposes, he wanted his disciples to go into the world to do the same. Since I was a serious follower of Christ, just as the disciples were, I assumed that his purpose for them must become my purpose—to use my life to reach others for him and to teach them what it meant to know and follow him by understanding and obeying his Word!

A last passage seemed to clinch this idea for me. Matthew 28:19-20 was a final command from Jesus to his disciples: "Go therefore and make disciples of all the nations, baptizing them in the name of the Father and the Son and Holy Spirit, teaching them to observe all that I commanded you; and lo, I am with you always, even to the end of the age."

Jesus wasn't asking his disciples to go into all the world and set up church buildings or youth groups or Wednesday night church suppers but to make disciples—to cultivate spiritual relationships with people, to draw them to Christ and then train them to reach out to other people who would also be trained and able to make other disciples. He was entrusting the messages and work of the kingdom of God into the hands of ordinary people who had come to know his love and forgiveness. The process of discipleship that Jesus modeled had become a reality in my own life. What Jesus had done with his disciples—living with them, loving them, forgiving them, instructing them, training them, serving them, and thereby transforming the whole foundations of their lives, my friends had done for me. And I knew I wanted to do the same with my life.

Ten years later, after having worked on staff for Campus Crusade as a missionary in Eastern Europe, and then in missions with Clay, I began my journey of motherhood. And I believe it was sometime during the first week of Sarah's life, as I held her tenderly in my arms thinking the sweet thoughts of a new mother, that I realized she was to become my own, in-home disciple in the making. I had spent the last ten years of my life in the ministry of making disciples from people I met in the world. Now Sarah and any future children would become the focus of my ministry. What an awesome realization it was that God had entrusted this precious little soul into my hands to seek to influence for his kingdom, so that she could become his disciple and continue passing the baton of righteousness to others who came into her life.

So when Sarah at age eighteen began to seek the answers to her own life's needs, I understood a little of what she was going through. I knew the struggle to find a mature and authentic faith, to find out where she fit in the world and the role God had for her to play in his kingdom. However, there was a big difference between Sarah's first steps into maturity and mine, because Sarah had a head start. From the time she was a baby, Clay and I had intentionally sought to disciple her. By God's grace, we had lived with her, instructed and corrected her, loved her, shown her firsthand what loving God looks like. We had deliberately followed Jesus' example as we trained her in spiritual disciplines. We knew the soil of her spirit had been tilled and planted with seeds of truth and righteousness, and we had already seen those seeds begin to sprout and grow. So we trusted that as she began to embrace Christianity for herself as an adult, the way would be familiar.

Now was the time for Sarah to begin drawing upon the resources we had built into her life so that she could strengthen her own muscles of faith and live out her own testimony. How exciting it has been for me as a parent to see the Lord's faithfulness in these aspirations. This year, the Lord has started a bright fire in Sarah's heart to live for his purposes and his kingdom. Her desire to share her faith with others and to have a ministry of her own has grown and matured. Her spiritual life has deepened as she has sought God for real answers to her life's questions and come to conclusions that have astounded and delighted me.

How amazed and thankful I am to see God producing in all my children's lives a love for him and a maturity that could be cultivated only by the Holy Spirit. It all started naturally in our own home as we sought to follow God's pattern for discipleship shown through the life of Christ. I am convinced it was all a part of his plan to use my home as a place of ministry.

It was part of God's plan that I recruit my own children to drop the fishing nets of their own lives in order to embrace God's purpose and mission.

It all began when I was able to embrace with joy the ministry of motherhood. But it didn't happen without some glitches along the way. Even though I knew a lot about ministry, the ministry of motherhood was something completely new to me.

A PLAN—AND A MODEL

It was half past five in the morning, and the darkness of night felt like a thick cloud hovering over my mind and body. But as I opened my eyes, I realized what had stirred me out of my deep sleep. The hungry cry of my sweet giant of a baby boy was now demanding my full attention. I had no desire to have little Nathan's cries awaken his brother and sister; I was hoping for a few moments alone before the bustle of a new day spilled over my exhausted body. So I quickly jumped out of bed, tiptoed to his side, and gently picked him up.

I changed his diaper, sat down with him in the old, squishy overstuffed recliner, and began to nurse him, hoping he would soon be satisfied and fall deeply back to sleep. But just as I was gingerly laying him back in the crib so as not to disturb his deep, slumbering breathing, little two-and-a-half-year-old Joel burst into the room with a deeply troubled face and squealing voice.

"Mommy, come quick! I've had diadeeda, and ith's all over my sheets, and it thmells weally bad!"

Weariness descended upon my body like a heavy cloak as Nathan wailed his objection to being so rudely awakened. I took Joel firmly by the arm and said in a louder-than-necessary voice, "I will be with you in just a minute. Go back to the bathroom right now, and never, ever come into a room and talk loudly when a baby is sleeping!"

He turned away slowly with a pathetic look on his little face and walked out of the room with half his diaper hanging off his skinny bottom. I quickly nursed Nathan back to sleep, laid him back in the crib, and quietly closed his door, hoping against hope that he would stay asleep.

Maybe, I thought as I slowly walked up the stairs to Joel's bedroom, it wasn't such a good idea to come to Clay's mom's house for a visit—not with three children under six years of age and without Clay. The physical strain of such a task was frazzling my nerves.

I changed the sheets, changed Joel's diaper, and looked for the Pepto-Bismol, at which point Sarah ran into Joel's room frantically holding her nose. "Mommy, there's something gross all over my bed and it smells, and I'm having one of my famous nosebleeds like I always do when we come to Texas…"

The evidence of Joel's having visited Sarah's room before my own was mingled all over her bed with the profusion of blood that had covered her sheets. I commanded Sarah to lie down in my bed. I pulled her sheets off the bed and piled them up with Joel's. I then administered an icepack to her nose and told her to "lie still!"

Over the next couple of hours, I put Nathan back to sleep two more times. I tripped over the cat, who had wrapped his tail around my legs while I was standing in front of the washer in the garage, trying to get the spots out of the sheets. I burned the French toast. Clay's mom told me the air conditioner seemed to be broken. (It was Sunday in Texas in August, the temperature was supposed to be 104 that day, and I hate heat!) I changed two more diarrhea diapers and, just as Sarah's nose started profusely bleeding again, I heard Joel say, "Uh-oh, Mommy!" I turned around to find him looking down at a bottle of pink Pepto-Bismol that he had spilled all over my mother-in-law's living room carpet. I remember looking at my watch and gasping as I saw that it was only half past nine—still almost four hours until naptime! Four hours until any hope of a reprieve.

All these things really did happen, and I had come to Texas to get away from some of the stress and strain I was feeling in California!

We had moved two years before to the Los Angeles area, where Clay had taken a position at a large church to work in discipleship ministry with older singles and develop the small groups in the church. The expectation was that he would work sixty to seventy hours a week. That left me at home to raise our children pretty much alone. All three of them were plagued with respiratory infections, ear infections, and asthma, which sometimes required hospitalization. I spent much of my time in doctors' offices, trying to placate my three little ones as I waited for our appointment. Many nights I hardly slept because of a hungry nursing baby and my other two sickly children, who seemed to need me most often in the middle of the night.

Even in the midst of feeling terribly alone with the pressure of tending to my small children, I had received various negative lectures about the choices I had made for my life and family. When we had a third child, for instance, one of my "Job's friends" had challenged me. I already had a girl and a boy. Didn't I realize that children were expensive? I didn't need to complicate life by having a third child.

Another critic reminded me that of ten staff families at church, I was the only mom who wasn't employed outside the home. Did I realize what financial pressure I was placing on my husband by staying home with the children?

I had not been prepared for the fast-paced, expensive lifestyle in

Southern California—or for the fact that family seemed to have definitely lost its importance in the values there. Of the twelve adult leaders in one of our small discipleship groups, eleven came from broken homes.

It was around this time that Sarah, age five, came to me and said, "Mom, you know, I think when I get my divorce, I'll just move back in with you and Daddy!" So many of the people we loved and worked with were divorced that Sarah assumed divorce was something to be expected.

As a young mother with three children age five and under, I would come to the end of each day wondering what I had accomplished. Between putting meals on the table, washing clothes, picking up toys, settling fusses, and all the other multitudinous tasks that took up my day, I sometimes felt I was digressing in my life instead of becoming more productive. My mother-heart wanted so much to give my precious children the best in life—even to disciple them the way I had been discipled. Instead, I felt I was actually losing ground.

I realized with the passing of each day that spiritual and emotional maturity would not just happen to my children because I wished it so. It would not come just from a passive example of my being good. Effective spiritual, emotional, and social training in the lives of my children would have to be both intentional and planned.

When Clay and I began to talk about these issues, we decided we needed a map or plan to help us make a positive spiritual impact on our children's lives. And as the primary caregiver, I especially needed something to guide me through my busy days and help me evaluate the ministry potential of what I was doing at any given moment. I knew the process of discipleship with adults because of years of working with them. But how, in the midst of my harried life, could I apply what I had learned to the lives of my children?

The light started to dawn when we talked about gifts—what we wanted to give our kids to last their whole lives. As we talked, we reflected that we wanted to give our children the real gifts of life that God had given us—humbling grace, life-changing love, a sense of meaning and purpose, and especially an intangible, internal faith in him and his Word that would never fail in any situation and could never be taken away.

But even more, we wanted our children to also *be* gifts of God's grace and love to a fallen world. We wanted them to carry on the mission of making him known in the world, as we had taken it on as young believers. We wanted to pass on the baton of righteousness to our children, so to speak, so they could pass on these gifts of life to future generations.

As Clay and I discussed our heartfelt convictions and ideas into the wee hours of many nights, we gradually came up with a plan or outline that has carried us through the training of our children for their whole lives. Originally we called our plan "Mother Gifts," because it grew out of my need to be sure I was reaching my goals with my children. Later, as we refined our plan, it became "Life Gifts," because we realized that passing on a spiritual heritage was a goal for both of us, not just for me.

Our plan was not a formula or program but a set of principles—a kind of checklist to help us remember our family ministry goals. We used the word GIFTS as an acronym to help us remember the spiritual priorities in our children's training.

Once Clay and I spelled out this parenting plan, I began to pray about how to implement it into our daily lives. This meant that as I lived out my days, in any given situation, I would ask myself lots of questions. I would think: How can I use this situation to give Sarah a greater understanding of God's grace or show Nathan how to give grace to Joel? Or: Can I use this situation to inspire Joy (our beloved "caboose," born when Sarah was

G represents the *gift of grace*—the kind of undeserved but freely given love and favor that comes from God. We model grace by extending it to our children but also by insisting that they learn to extend it to others. Practically speaking, the gift of grace is all about relationships. It's the desire and ability to relate personally and lovingly to God and people.

I represents the *gift of inspiration*—which is all about motivation and purpose. This gift is essentially the desire and ability to view all of life in the light of God's sovereignty and purpose. Inspiring my children to understand God's purpose for their lives and say yes to his call provides them with a sense of meaning. It helps gives them the energy they need to do what God wants in their lives.

F represents the *gift of faith*—both content and attitude. We give this gift both by teaching "the faith" (sound doctrine, biblical literacy, practical application) and by modeling what it means to live in faith, trusting God for our needs. Biblical faith gives my children the strength they need to proceed in their walk with the Lord. The gift of faith is the desire and ability to know God through his Word and Spirit and to trust him for every area of life.

T represents the *gift of training*—the desire and ability to grow in Christian maturity and godly character in the power of the Holy Spirit. It's not just telling children how to live, not just modeling right behavior, but repeating these lessons with patience and perseverance until they become part of their lives. Training is a process of gradually moving a child's character and habits in a godly direction.

S represents the *gift of service*—the desire and ability to minister God's grace and truth to others. Giving my children a heart for ministry teaches them how to serve God tangibly and practically by using their hearts and their hands for ministry.

eleven) with the idea of God's call on her life? Is there a scripture I can use to teach my children about God or his Word? Is this a situation in which I need to train my child's character or habits? Is this a situation in which I can show my child how to serve and reach out to someone else?

Keeping the GIFTS idea in mind as I went about my daily tasks helped me a lot. But I still found myself floundering sometimes, and one question often led to another. What I really needed was a practical model to help me apply our plan to my daily life.

Then the obvious answer struck me: Jesus was the model I was looking for.

A big part of his ministry, after all, was teaching his disciples—just as I had been taught in that campus ministry and just as I was trying to teach my children. He ministered to them, and he prepared them for ministry. He taught them with his words, and he taught them with his actions. Jesus gave his disciples—and my mentors gave me—the very gifts Clay and I wanted to give our children.

How did he do it? How did he establish them in their faith so that after he died each one of them fully embraced his call on their lives to love and serve him? That's what I needed to learn. So, as I had my quiet times or read Scripture, I began to jot down specific thoughts and ideas about how Jesus led his disciples into ministry and how I could do the same for my children. As I became aware of the leadership principles he used with his own disciples, I recorded them under my GIFTS outline. They became the principles I would pass to my own children.

My personal reward for this study has been far greater than I could have imagined. It has led me to a much deeper faith and a deeper understanding of the integrity of his life. It has fueled my passion to love and know him better. My understanding of his boundless love and commitment has been a source of strength that has kept me going forward. His life has also become my model for how to be a godly mother.

The combination of my GIFTS plan and my study of Jesus' life gave me a very practical guide for implementing eternal goals in my everyday life with my four children. As I have revisited these ideas over the years— my children now range in age from nine to twenty—I have had many opportunities to pass them on to other moms who want to train their children how to walk their own spiritual journey. Many mothers have written to ask me to put my experience in print—to pass along what I have learned about discipling my children Jesus' way and passing along his gifts to them.

This book is my answer to those requests. In a sense, it's my gift to you—from one mother to another. Because I know you're busy, it's written in short chapters based on the GIFTS outline that helped me so much. Most of the chapters are thoughtful and devotional in nature, drawn from episodes in my own life. But because the life of Jesus is my model for the ministry of motherhood, I've chosen to begin each section with an imaginative re-creation from the life of Christ—a dramatic retelling that shows how our Lord gave the gifts of grace, inspiration, faith, training, and service to those he loved. I hope these stories will inspire you as they have inspired me.

How you read this book depends on you. It's designed to work either as a six-week personal or small-group study or as a less structured resource for thought and reflection.

If you're interested in the six-week study, I recommend you spend the first week on this introduction, using the study questions at the end to help you clarify your own ideas and ministry goals before you proceed with the rest of the book. After that, you can proceed with one "gift" section each week. Begin the week with the chapter that reflects on Jesus' model of teaching and equipping. Read one of the three accompanying meditations on each of the following days. On the fifth day, work through the study and discussion questions, or just spend the time looking back over the section, meditating on how the "gift" you have been reading about might apply to your life. On the remaining two days, take a break, or meet with your group for encouragement and support.

If you prefer to read this book more casually, dipping into the chapters as you find the time, you'll find that each chapter can stand alone as a kind of daily devotion. It's not necessary to read the "gifts" in the order I've presented them, and the meditation chapters can be interchanged as well. But I do recommend that you begin each "gift" section with the first chapter and that you finish one "gift" before starting another, allowing time for the full possibilities of ministry through grace, inspiration, faith, training, or service to permeate your thoughts and your prayers.

In Luke 6:40, we read, "A pupil is not above his teacher; but everyone, after he has been fully trained, will be like his teacher." Our children are, in a sense, our pupils in life. When they are fully trained, they will be like us, their teachers. How assuring it is, then, to be able to follow the pattern of our own great Teacher's life as we are training them. All those moments in our lives—and in our children's lives—become eternally meaningful as we live out the reality of the ministry of motherhood. In so doing, we truly give our children an eternal gift—the gift of knowing and following the Lord who gives us everything.

For Study and Discussion

Your Ministry of Motherhood

1. What purpose do you think God had in mind when he designed the role of mother? Have you ever specifically considered that, in becoming a mother, you have actually been called to a ministry? In what way does that concept change how you think about your role?

2. Read Psalm 127:3—if possible, in more than one translation. What does this verse imply about the ministry of motherhood?

3. Proverbs 31:10-31 paints a vivid portrait of the life of a godly woman. Describe what a Proverbs 31 life might look like in a modern context. What parts of this description do you find particularly inspiring? Which areas pose a challenge for you? How do you think these reactions relate to your ministry as a mother?

4. Read Proverbs 14:1. In what specific ways can a woman in this day and age build her house or tear it down? If possible, give examples from your own observation or experience. Then list four specific ways you want to build your house by ministering to your children and making disciples of them.

5. Write out a plan for ministering to your own children using the acronym GIFTS. List at least one goal for each letter.

PART ONE

The Gift of Grace

If it were possible to take all that Christ was and is—his mercy and love, his righteousness and holiness, his power and intelligence, his creativity and wisdom—and focus all of it for the benefit of an undeserving person, we would begin to have a sense of what God's grace is all about. We would also have to consider the world he has made for us—the beautiful and colorful sights of nature; the sounds we hear and hum; food to taste and smell; the sensation of touch on our skin; and ideas expressed through words such as *love, freedom, self-sacrifice,* and *purpose.* The multifaceted expression of God's greatness through what he made was a gift of grace to us at the beginning of time to show us his love and favor. Then, after we humans rebelled and fell away from God, he sent his Son to redeem a fallen world back to himself that we might personally still know him in his fullness. This was the fullness of his grace—God's undeserved favor toward us. His serving us in generous love through a loving, humble relationship introduces us to the essence of his personality. His grace changes our lives and is the foundation for our learning to give grace to others in our relationships.

*Grace leads us to know God and his unconditional love
and to extend it to others.*

Chapter 1

Out of the Boat— a Model for Grace

It was dawn over the Sea of Galilee, cool and blue, and the sun was barely glowing on the horizon. A fresh wind danced over the water and blended with the sweet, new air of morning as awakening birds sang their welcome to the sun. A few gentle waves rippled over the sea, dark blue at first, then iridescent green and shimmering gold as the sun rose. A profusion of light and color filled the sky, pouring through the clouds in crimson, violet, and gold, and the new day appeared in its full glory.

In the middle of the sea, silhouetted against the rising sun, floated a small fishing boat. The waves rocked it gently, and the water sparkled on the fishing net trailing loosely behind it. But all the beauty was lost to the man sitting hunched and weary in the prow of the boat. His shoulders were bent, and his eyes, dark with exhaustion and sorrow, stared down at the damp floor of the boat. Simon Peter was oblivious to the sunny morning because a storm was raging in his soul.

It had been several weeks since the remarkable day when Jesus had risen. But all Peter could think about now was that awful night before the Lord died, the night when he, Peter, the one Jesus had called Cephas, or "the rock," had denied he ever knew his Master. He had been a coward of the worst sort, deserting the Son of God in his greatest hour of need. He felt he could never escape the shame or the guilt that washed over him every time he thought about it.

What's the use? he wondered. What good was he to Jesus now? He had been so sure of the future before that terrible day the Master died. But now, even though Jesus had come to life, Peter was drowning in despair. If only he could live that evening over again!

"Are you still moping, Peter?" It was John's voice, speaking from the bow of the boat. "You've got to get past this. You know the Lord forgave you. And everything's different now anyway. Think of it. The Lord is alive!"

Peter did know that—and it didn't help. Oh, he was glad that Jesus had risen, had come back to life in perfect triumph and glory. For a little while, Peter had even felt forgiven and reassured. When Jesus embraced him that first time after the resurrection, Peter had been confident all was well. He would have died for Jesus on the spot! But in the days since, when Jesus had not reappeared, the guilt had returned. Day by day it had grown in his mind, reminding him of his failure, stealing his joy and power. Sometimes it felt as though someone were standing in the corridors of his mind, pointing a finger of accusation at all his thoughts.

If only he could see the Master again, he thought, then everything would be all right. He could show the Lord that he really did believe in him and love him. But who knew when he would see Jesus? John was right. Everything was different now…

A breaking bubble in the water drew Peter's attention back to his fishing. Peering over the side of the boat, Peter reached down to shake the net. Still empty. With a disgusted look on his face, he flung the net back in the water and heaved a long, deep sigh.

"I can't even fish anymore," he muttered. "I'm good for nothing, nothing at all!"

He turned to steer the boat shoreward. There was no use waiting anymore; the fish just weren't there. As he began to roll up the rope, though, his attention was drawn to the shore. A man was standing there, just a dim figure on the distant sand but somehow familiar. And he was waving and calling out to their boat.

"Children,"—the man's voice was strong and friendly—"have you caught no fish this morning?"

"None at all, sir!" called back John.

"Try casting your nets on the other side," called the man. "See what it will bring you."

Peter could have sworn he caught a note of laughter in the command.

Shrugging his shoulders at John, Peter set to work. It certainly couldn't hurt; nothing else they had tried had worked. And he felt a sort of childlike curiosity to see if it would make a difference. So he helped John and James pull the nets up and carry them to the other side, the shoreward side, dropping them in and carelessly poking down the ends.

A moment passed. Peter was about to give up. It was a crazy idea anyhow. Then suddenly the hand holding the end of the net was jerked down, and the mesh sank deeply into the water as the squirming, shiny bodies of hundreds of fish poured in.

But Peter had forgotten all about the fish when he looked up again. Why hadn't he seen it before?

John saw it too. "It is the Lord," he said. But Peter didn't hear him. He had already jumped into the water.

"I'm coming, Master!" Peter yelled before his head went under. His arms pushed powerfully through the water, and in the few minutes it took him to swim ashore he felt as if the whole world had changed. Jesus was there. Jesus would make everything right. If Peter could just be with Jesus, he would do anything, *could* do anything! He swam faster as excitement poured through him. It was as if an invisible cord were tied around his heart and connected to Jesus, and the cord pulled him to his Master.

He reached the shore. Slipping on the sand, he stumbled up the beach and then fell at Jesus' feet.

"Master, oh Master! You're here!"

Jesus reached down and put a strong, loving arm over Peter's shoulders. Peter looked up into eyes that were full of joy, laughter, and a love that absolved all guilt. The light of grace shone in Jesus' eyes as though to say, "It's all right. My life and love will cover all of your darkness. Just depend on me. You are my chosen one."

"Come on, Peter!" the Lord was saying. "I've made breakfast for you; it must have been a long night of fishing!"

So Peter followed, and as he walked, he suddenly became aware of the sunlight dancing on the water, the wind that whispered around him and dried his clothes. The rising sun seemed to shine right down into his heart, and he knew the glory of the morning. The Master had come, and once again his heart was filled with hope. Jesus, the one who once called him to become "a fisher of men" had reminded him again that, at his direction, all things would be possible.[1]

From the very beginning of their time together, Jesus called his disciples to a life apart from the crowd. He called them to great purpose and meaning, promising to make them "fishers of men." But even before that, he called them into a relationship with him. He extended to them the grace of his fellowship, his love, his instruction. With them he was patient, encouraging, loving, and forgiving. His whole relationship with them was built on the foundation of intimate friendship. He gave them the gift of *himself.* And then he asked them to pass along that gift to the world.

We see this more and more clearly as Jesus' relationship with the disciples progressed. He wanted them to be his representatives on earth, to tell everyone the gospel of the kingdom of his Father. But he wanted them to do it through his strength and grace, not through their own power. And this was where Peter got it wrong.

Peter was a strong, active man. He was used to making decisions, being dependable. It was natural for him to assume that by his great effort he would "help" the Lord get his message to the world. Yet Jesus, knowing the need of Peter's heart, allowed him to find out differently. He allowed Peter to fail spectacularly so he would finally understand that grace was the key to serving God and his kingdom. Not by his own strength and courage, but only by God's constant grace and mercy would Peter be able to deliver Jesus' message to the world—a message that would then be wrapped in the grace and mercy he had come to know so well.

As mothers, I believe, we are called to take this lesson of grace to heart. Like Jesus, we are to draw our own children to a life apart from the rest of the crowd. Each of us is designed by God to whisper his words to the hearts of our children so they will feel the call of God in their own lives to become "fishers of men." Yet we must always remember that our children, like Peter, will never be perfect. Each of them needs for us, like Jesus, to extend to him or her the gift of constant love, grace, and forgiveness. And we can only do this by relying continually on the grace of our own relationship with the Lord.

When we do this, we will live out the definition of grace and love in such a way that our message will be written on their hearts. They will understand that the God who calls them to a great task will stay with them as they strive to complete it. They will know he gives them the strength and encouragement they need—and the grace to pick themselves up when they fall. And they will know all this in part because of the hands-on grace they have experienced at home.

Giving the gift of grace to our children is actually a two-part process. First, we need to help our children *receive* grace. We do this both by extending grace to them and by teaching them about God's grace through salvation. After that, by our teaching and example, we must train our children to *give* grace to others in turn.

Jesus summed up this two-part process when he was asked to name the greatest commandment. He said we are first to love the Lord God with all our hearts (receiving grace), and then we are to love our neighbors as ourselves (giving grace). This commandment, therefore, sums up the first gift we can give to our children—the desire and ability to understand and receive the grace of God and to give it to the rest of the world.

Understanding the importance of the gift of grace has really helped me respond to the daily dilemmas and frustrations of life in a household of four children. As we go through our days, for instance, I try to be mindful that, to God, relationships are always a top priority. I try to think of ways I can model for my children the redemptive grace and love of Jesus—and also influence them to extend grace to others through their actions and their attitudes.

In all of this, however, I must acknowledge, as Peter learned, that it's not all up to me. The Author of grace will himself draw my children to him, even as he did Peter, as I rest in his ability to work through the life of my family. Perfection is not a standard he requires of me as a mother, for his grace extends to me as well as to my children. My heartfelt trust in him will be the fuel that energizes my days as I see him draw my children through this gift that will serve them their whole lives.

Chapter 2

The Grace of
Time Together

Half past ten in the evening found me downstairs, dragging my weary body on a tour of my four children's bedrooms to say good night. I had been up since four that morning, and all I could think of was my own bed and how I longed for sleep. Nathan's room was my last stop, and I hoped for a quick good-night so I could finally be through with this stress-filled day.

It was the Christmas season in a new home. All four of my children were lonely, missing the familiarity of friends and the flurry of activity that normally comes with the Christmas bustle. (Leaving beautiful Colorado had not been a popular decision.) But thirteen-year-old Nathan, in his extroverted, adolescent-hormone-filled body, had been hit the hardest. He missed his best friend and next-door neighbor, Michael, and he was letting all of us know it. Though he has a heart of gold and was trying hard to use

31

self-control, he had a puppy-dog look in his blue eyes that begged for attention. To be honest, I didn't think I had it in me. I felt drained and wrung out just trying to keep all four children happy and cared for in their restless need for more than I had to give.

I sat on Nathan's bed, prayed a quick good-night prayer, said a hasty "see you in the morning, honey," and bolted for the door in hopes of making a quick retreat to my room. After all, I had fulfilled my obligation as a good mom to "tuck in" all of my children.

Then Nathan's pleading voice quietly taunted me.

"Don't you even have a few minutes that we can talk?"

I mustered my own self-control, sat back down on his bed, and tried hard not to show my desire to leave as quickly as possible.

"What do you want to talk about?" I queried.

"Oh, nothing. I just wanted someone to be with."

"How about I scratch your back?"

He turned over on his bed, and I slowly began to "soft tickle" his back, a phrase coined by our family when Sarah was a little girl. As I began this labor of love, questions, thoughts, ideas, and dreams started pouring out of Nathan's mouth. The longer I scratched his freckled back, the more he seemed to relax.

"I hope someone will ask me to do a magic show at a birthday party soon, Mom. Do you think anyone will see the fliers I put up?... What are we going to do tomorrow?... Do you think we can have an open house for all the neighbors on Sunday?... When do you think we can take a trip back to Colorado? I can't wait for the Dallas conference so I can see Michael and all my friends!... Mom, don't you think Kelsey is a good dog? She doesn't mean to be so wild; she's just a puppy. Sort of like me, I guess.... What do you think we should get Joel for Christmas?… Do you really think I'm a good writer?"

One thought spilled into another as the minutes ticked away. And I could feel my irritation gradually draining away too. I couldn't help thinking how blessed I was to have a teenage child who wanted to share the company of his frumpy mother.

When the spilling out of Nathan's heart seemed to be slowing down, I did one final flurry of scratching his back and then pulled down his T-shirt to close this time of sweet fellowship, which would be in my memory forever.

"Thanks for taking the time, Mom," Nathan said as he gently reached up to kiss my cheek. "It meant a lot to me."

I once had dreams of great feats I wanted my children to accomplish with their lives. I wanted them to have a strong moral character and be a testimony for Christ. I wanted them to be leaders to their lost and wandering friends. I wanted them to be excellent in their manners and conduct, work habits, and schoolwork and to be gracious and patient to each other. I wanted them to take up their cross and follow hard after Christ in whatever they were asked to do.

I still have those dreams, of course. But I've also realized that my dreams are not necessarily what really motivate my children to become the best they can be. What matters to them is my loving presence. Nathan wanted me to be his friend, someone who would take the time to talk and scratch his back. And that's what all my children need from me. If I want them to be open to my messages, I need to be willing to serve them—to voluntarily give up my rights and my time to meet their felt needs—just as Jesus was willing to give for his disciples.

The night before Jesus was to be crucified, his heart and mind must have been filled with weariness and exhaustion at the thought of what he would soon endure. The sins of the whole world—throughout all of history!—were about to be placed upon his back as he laid down his life to pay the penalty for all of us. He knew he would be rejected by those who loved him. He would be beaten and scourged, spit upon, and wrongly sacrificed in the most demeaning way upon a cross while being handled by rough and sneering Roman soldiers.

Yet it is at this point that we see him making a beautiful gesture of love and service toward his disciples:

> Now before the Feast of the Passover, Jesus knowing that His
> hour had come that He would depart out of this world to the
> Father, having loved His own who were in the world, He loved
> them to the end.... Jesus, knowing that the Father had given all
> things into His hands, and that He had come forth from God
> and was going back to God, got up from supper, and laid aside
> His garments; and taking a towel, He girded Himself. Then He
> poured water into the basin, and began to wash the disciples'
> feet and to wipe them with the towel with which He was
> girded. (John 13:1,3-5)

Jesus was about to ask his disciples to do the same thing he was doing—to sacrifice their lives for his kingdom. He also knew each would be required to die for his kingdom as he was about to do. He was going to transfer to them the responsibility of taking God's message of redemptive love to the world. But instead of just telling them what to do, harshly commanding their allegiance with orders and threats or guilt and manipulative statements, he chose to tie the cords of his heart to theirs with the strong and unbreakable bond of a loving, serving relationship.

Jesus spent his last night on earth with his disciples in service to them. How powerful their memories of that night must have been—the King of the whole universe touching and rubbing their dusty feet and gently drying them with a towel. Their Lord and Master breaking the loaf of bread and serving each of them for the celebrated feast of the Passover.

Jesus' example of servant leadership sets him apart from so many historical religious leaders. He was not a God who lorded it over his followers and demanded they follow him or coerced their obedience through authoritarianism and fear. Instead, he called them to the excellence of holiness and yet lovingly served them in order to win their hearts and show them the means of reaching others' hearts as well.

As I look to the hearts of my own children and seek to teach them about the grace of God, I realize my love and service to them must come before any of my great words, my teaching and training. My time, my attention, my "soft-tickling"—even when I am tired or have other "important" things on my mind—is what builds our relationship and prepares them to listen to what I have to say. Only then, once the wells of their need are filled with the grace of being loved, will my words to them about God's grace finally make sense.

Human cultures have always tended to see leadership in terms of authority or power. The one who is in charge is the one who sits behind the desk and has people serve him. But Jesus showed us the power of a different kind of leadership. He lived with his disciples. He was with them when they were joking, tired, angry, clever, questioning. He walked with them in the presence of Pharisees and religious leaders as well as in the quiet of their own homes. They were with him when he healed the blind and cast out demons and when he gave up precious hours of sleep to pray to the Father. In observing the whole of his life—his constant focus on his Father, his compassion and energy to serve every possible kind of human being (prostitutes, Samaritans, Jews, and Romans; children, women, and men; the poor and wealthy), his strength and integrity in everyday moments—they began to build a true understanding of what walking with God looked like in real flesh. It was because of Jesus' total life commitment to them, their friendship with them, and his willingness to give to them— his time, his wisdom, his practical help, even cutting short his precious prayer time to rescue them from predicaments such as a tossing boat—that they were able to respond in return, giving their whole lives to him.

The longer I have been a mom, the more I see this principle to be true. Though Clay and I do have family devotions and regular times of individual prayer with our children, we also work alongside them doing chores at home. We take them with us as we prepare for church dinners or teach Bible studies or help in soup kitchens. Participating with us in our conferences as we speak and serve and provide music has provided many life memories. We keep them accountable in their schoolwork and take time to read great stories together. We attend church as a group, just as we ski or go to movies together. Our children watch and notice Clay and me as we nurse them in their illnesses, correct them when they are rebellious, celebrate their accomplishments, arrange fun birthday breakfasts and holiday celebrations, and commiserate with them in their failures or conflict with friends. It's not just a matter of setting a good example. Our influence comes from our willingness to be with our children and to serve them on a day-to-day basis.

"Serving" children does not mean letting them order us around or giving in to all their whims. This was certainly not Jesus' example of servant leadership. The disciples were always clear who was the leader in their little band, and Jesus commanded their obedience. But he earned that obedience not by pulling rank but by putting their welfare second only to the will of his Father.

Sometimes we serve our children best and most lovingly by sticking to our guns and *not* letting them have their way. Loving discipline can be part of the gift of grace. So can teaching with words and exhorting our children to excellence. But the relationship has to come first. Discipline and teaching are most effective when administered in a context of a close, ongoing relationship of love.

Even last night, as I was about to go to sleep, the boys came into my room after playing tennis in the park and sat with me on my bed for thirty minutes, laughing and talking about the moments of their day. What a wonderful time of unplanned fellowship we had as we talked about church, difficult people, commitments we have failed in, and lessons they are learning. It was such a productive time, but I still had to have a servant heart in order to be willing to be available to them, to see it taking place. It would have been so easy to just close my door and say I was already almost asleep.

Passing on the gift of grace to our children requires a commitment—and yes, a sacrifice—of time, love, and heart service. The grace we give by serving our children will provide them with a pattern to follow the rest of their lives. When they relate to their own friends, bosses, neighbors, spouses, and children, the example of our lives will steer the decisions they make. The grace they show to others will largely come from parents who learned it first from our own servant King.

―A MOTHER'S PRAYER―

Most Gracious Lord,
Help us remember, in all the moments of our days, that taking time
to cultivate a close relationship with our children is what will open
their hearts for you. Give us strength and grace to listen to their
dreams, to comfort them in their sorrows, and to make ourselves
available for their needs. Help us remember that they want our
attention more than our service. Thank you that you made yourself
available to people and that you always make time for each of us.

Amen

Chapter 3

The Grace of Encouraging Words

Our new home in Lebanon, Tennessee, lies at the very eastern edge of the central time zone. This means that in winter the days are especially short. The sun sets by five o'clock, and the house begins to get dark even earlier. On one of these gloomy winter afternoons, I had sat down wearily to have a cup of tea before the last-blast effort of evening—fixing dinner and meeting everyone's nighttime needs so I could close another day. But the shadows of the fast-fading light seemed to envelop me in a melancholy cloud.

One more move, for the sake of our ministry, had brought our family to this little rural town near Nashville. We had consolidated three offices from other states, hoping to free up more time for ourselves as a family and as a couple. But the move had proved to be disastrous at every level, and I felt my inadequacies at every turn.

The children missed their friends and our mountain home in Colorado. The new house had never quite been tamed in the months since our move; some orphan boxes still waited in the garage, having never been opened. We couldn't quite get to a regular schedule where the chores were completed, family devotions were consistent, and meals were on the table at the right time. Outside activities had proved to be less than satisfactory for each of us. I hadn't been able to find a good guitar or violin teacher, there was no young magicians club for Nathan, other classes seemed inadequate compared to what we used to have, and no church seemed quite a "fit." The smooth rhythms of life that usually provided stability to this crew of six seemed to elude us here. As a result, everyone seemed to need an extra dose of me, and the truth was, I didn't have a lot left to give.

It was at this moment that the phone rang to break the stillness of the room and to interrupt my morose thoughts.

"Hi, Sally! I just got your new book." The familiar voice of a dear friend immediately gave comfort to my heart. "I've been looking it over," she went on. "And, Sally, it is so powerful! I know the Lord is going to use it greatly to help many women and give them the hope they need to keep going. I believe the message is so important. Many mothers and many children will be changed because of reading this book. I just wanted to encourage you and let you know I was thinking about you!"

Within the few short moments my friend was on the line, I felt my heart flood with light and warmth. It was as though she had sung a melody of love over me and rekindled the music in my soul. Somehow her words reminded me that my effort to be a good mother and to encourage other moms was very significant. Her call gave me a reason to keep plugging through this difficult passage. It reminded me that what we were trying to do was worth the struggle.

Though I had never really doubted that the Lord was watching over our family and directing our paths, I needed to hear the encouragement aloud as well. So my friend became the voice of God for me in that moment. She took the initiative to speak words that gave me life. I was surprised how just that one call carried me emotionally through the next few weeks.

Words are powerful; the Bible is full of that message. The whole universe came into being because God spoke the words. God's written word in the form of Scripture is central to his ongoing communication with his people. Jesus himself, God's ultimate form of communication, is described as the Word of God. And the Bible is clear that our words are important too. Many verses instruct us in the importance of words spoken as a source of life and encouragement. A few of these verses from Proverbs describe how precious words can be:

> A soothing tongue is a tree of life. (15:4)

> A man has joy in an apt answer,
> And how delightful is a timely word! (15:23)

> Like apples of gold in settings of silver
> Is a word spoken in right circumstances. (25:11)

Encouraging and affirming words—words of life, as I like to call them—have the power to give hope, to strengthen others to keep growing in righteousness. And if I, a grown woman, need them to keep me going through hard times, my children need them even more. Positive words act as water and sunshine to our souls to help them grow strong. Yet I have found that very few people really take the time to say those words that all of us, and especially our children, long to hear.

"I love and appreciate you!"

"Your friendship means a lot to me!"

"I believe in you and in what God is doing in your life!"

"You are special to the Lord and to me, and I am praying for you."

Thinking good thoughts about someone doesn't really bless that person. We have to take the initiative actually to say the words—in person, through a card or e-mail, or even through a phone call.

As I look to the life of Jesus, I see that he constantly blessed people with his words. He often spoke encouragement and affirmation directly to those around him or affirmed them before others.

To the woman who had been hemorrhaging for twelve years, he said, "Daughter, take courage; your faith has made you well" (Matthew 9:22). Even as his touch healed her body, his encouraging words must have healed her heart.

As Mary of Bethany sat at Jesus' feet, he spoke words to her sister that were obviously intended for her ears as well: "Mary has chosen the good part, which shall not be taken away from her" (Luke 10:42). How good those words of support must have felt after she had just been scolded for her poor manners and faulty hospitality.

Jesus greeted Nathanael, whom he would call to be his follower, with strong words of praise: "Behold, an Israelite indeed, in whom is no deceit!" (John 1:47, NKJV).

And at least twice in the Gospels, we see Jesus pronouncing his favor and appreciation to women who anointed him. The first was a woman who was known to be a "sinner" (Luke 7:37-48). Jesus commended her in front of a Pharisee, which must have felt like affirmation indeed. The second time (which is mentioned twice, in Matthew 26:6-13 and Mark 14:9), Jesus commended the woman by promising her deed would be remembered "wherever this gospel is preached in the whole world" (Matthew 26:13). Imagine how she must have felt when he said that! Jesus truly had a spirit of appreciation, affirmation, and encouragement.

Jesus was especially careful to uplift and motivate his disciples with his words. From the beginning he spoke of their potential and their future, saying he would make them "fishers of men," that they would do great wonders, that he loved them just as the Father loved them. And he spoke individual words of blessing they never forgot:

"Blessed are you, Simon Barjona," he said to Peter, "because flesh and blood did not reveal this to you, but My Father who is in heaven. I also say to you that you are Peter, and upon this rock I will build My church; and the gates of Hades will not overpower it" (Matthew 16:17-18).

Now, imagine how special you would feel if Jesus himself affirmed that your insights were revealed to you by God. And then to have him call you a "rock" and say he would build his church on the solid foundation of your life—what confidence those words would inspire. What an anchor of hope it would provide in times of doubt to remember that Jesus had said such things about you. To have the Son of God choose you to lead his church would indeed be a solid foundation from which to minister. Such words would carry you through many a time of doubt.

Even on the last night before his crucifixion, Jesus built up his disciples with words of love, encouragement, and hope. All through that Upper Room Discourse, he poured out words of love, strength, and comfort that would carry them through the painful days to come and through their lives of service to him.

"Do not let your heart be troubled, nor let it be fearful," he told them

(John 14:27). He promised that though he was about to leave them, he would not leave them alone but would send "another Helper," the Holy Spirit, to be with them forever (14:16). He invited them to "abide" in him and "ask whatever you wish, and it will be done for you" (15:7). "You…have grief now," he acknowledged, "but I will see you again, and your heart will rejoice, and no one will take your joy away from you" (16:22). Above all, he assured them again and again that "the Father Himself loves you" (16:27). We can only imagine how those words must have echoed in the disciples' hearts through the difficult days to come, bringing them comfort and strength and hope in the midst of their pain.

But the Lord's loving, encouraging words were not reserved just for Jesus' disciples. They are preserved on the pages of God's Word to lift us up today. The whole Bible is filled with words that have given strength, encouragement, hope, faith, and forgiveness to believers in all times and all ages. God's encouraging words are so powerful, in fact, that untold numbers of people who read them have loved God, served his kingdom purposes, and died for his cause.

Words matter! They have the power mysteriously to enter our hearts and minds and lift us beyond the present moment into the presence of God himself. How important it is, then, that we mothers, shepherds of our children's lives and hearts, choose our words to them carefully. We must deliberately aim our words at their hearts in such a way as to give our children hope, faith, strength, and also to point them toward the redeeming love of Christ. We can become the affirming voice of God to our children, just as we become a picture of his redeeming reality in their everyday lives. In this way we extend the gift of grace.

And we must never forget that our words can have a negative as well as a positive effect. The book of James makes this graphically clear when the writer talks about the power of the tongue: "From the same mouth come both blessing and cursing" (3:10). Words can be used to kill the spirit as well as to give life.

I'm not just talking about obvious verbal abuse. Cursing at children or telling them they're worthless can certainly be harmful. But a parent who would *never* use words in such extreme ways can still "curse" a child with words. For instance, we can be so committed to training our children that we use most of our words to correct and admonish them: "Do this!" "Stop that!" "Change that attitude!" I know I have been guilty of this at times. Words of instruction and training are indeed necessary to our children, but we must be careful not to discourage them through nagging, criticism, and reprimands. Even more important, we must balance our correction with words of encouragement and affirmation, words that our precious little ones will treasure in their hearts throughout their whole lives.

I have found that the teenage years for boys can be just as emotionally volatile as they are for girls. We have noticed that both of our boys have had extreme mood swings and big attitudes when they hit puberty. It was in the middle of one of those hormonal storms that one of my sons seemed bent on being sarcastic (which we try to correct), sassy (which is also not allowed), and angrily frustrated while doing household chores that had been a part of his routine his whole life. After a parent-child confrontation, this son stormed to his room for refuge and closed the door.

A few minutes later, I knocked on his door. My cup of hot chocolate was accepted only reluctantly. But as I sat down and asked if he wanted to talk, the tears began to flow.

"Mom, I'm so frustrated. I seem to get in trouble all the time. I can't seem to control my temper, and I don't really feel like I'm a very likable person."

He began to recite his weaknesses and faults and struggles as if reading a list he had reviewed mentally many times before. And as he did, I realized what I needed to do. I waited for him to finish, then I began to give him my own list of why I considered him to be a very special person.

"You are such a lover of people," I said, "and always so generous with your encouragement. I know the Lord is going to use you to give hope to many people. You are so gifted at writing and communicating ideas. Maybe you will write some great books. You are such an excellent performer and speaker. You are a natural. Your strong spirit in God's hands will be used to reach out to thousands. You are gifted at music, and you are creative and innovative, with lots of ideas about ways to do things. You are the biggest source of humor in our whole family, and your enthusiasm for activity has given all of us lots of fun and adventures that we would have missed. I can't even imagine how dull my life would be without you. You have always been very special to me, and I am quite sure God has a very special place for you in the world."

With each word I could see tension begin to melt away from my son like pieces of ice. He looked up at me with vulnerable, tender eyes and said, "Mom, do you really believe in me? You're not just saying these things?"

At that moment I was very aware of holding his fragile, open heart in my hands. I assured him once again of his great worth in the eyes of the King—and in my eyes as well. He sat up, put his arms around me in a bear hug, and said, "Mom, I love you so much! I don't know what I would do without your encouragement."

A day that had been filled with the tension of four growing children and two imperfect but sincere parents ended in peace. How thankful I am that God had shown me the way through his life-giving Word and the example of Jesus with his disciples years before. The lessons of his life will be passed down to my children's children because they became a pattern learned through the moments of life in our home as we sought to give our own children the gift of grace through our life-giving words.

—A MOTHER'S PRAYER—

Father of Encouragement,
Thank you for taking the time to show love to your disciples by affirming and encouraging them. Help us remember that our well-aimed words will carry life to the hearts of our children. Teach us to extol their positive characteristics whenever we can and to resist the temptation to use words only for correction. Give us lips that speak grace and that show the heart of your love through the things we say.
Amen

Chapter 4

The Grace of
Forgiveness in Action

I t seemed like such a good idea to let each of my children have a friend over to celebrate New Year's Eve in our home. We provided an abundance of delicious junk food, time-consuming board games, and favorite movies. It was an evening of fun and frenzy as our crowd of young people filled the house with their antics and energy.

The next day, however, with the last guest out the door, little Joy seemed out of sorts. A growing frown clouded her face. As the day progressed, I made several attempts to have her with me—while making lunch, reading together in the afternoon, and going outside for a quick winter's-day walk. Our conversations were short and stunted, interrupted by phone calls, children wanting to eat, a neighborhood dog attacking our own dog, who was in heat—the typical interesting and demanding minutes of life that occupy a family each day. But I had managed to be with

49

her and my other three children as they all tried to recover from staying up way too late.

That evening after dinner the older children wanted to watch a video that would have been enjoyable to me as well. But as we began the show, I realized the subject matter would be of little interest to Joy, who had come up to crawl into my lap. Her lanky seven-year-old body almost didn't fit anymore, and I was thankful there were special times when she was still willing to say, "Mom, I need your attention" by nuzzling in that way.

The Lord seemed to gently push my heart. Joy was growing up so quickly, and I realized I wanted to treasure such moments, which I knew from experience would pass in just a few years. So I suggested that she and I go down to her room, snuggle up on her bed, and watch a Shirley Temple movie called *Curly Top*.

"Oh, Mommy!" she responded. "Let's do it!"

I hooked up our small TV-VCR on the desk chair next to her bed. We squeezed in together among the pillows on her twin bed to talk, draw pictures, and watch this show, which never failed to delight her. But even before the video began, she began to fairly bubble over with things to say to me. And then I began to understand the reason for her daylong frown.

"Mommy, I feel bad about some things that happened with Ann last night. I've been worrying about it all day, but I didn't want the other kids to hear what I did. I haven't been able to think about anything else."

She proceeded to tell me that she and her friend had taken all the money out of her bank. They had hidden it in a backpack and gone out to the back of our three-acre yard to have an adventure. And somehow, as they counted the money and played with it, they had lost two of the collector coins that were precious to her.

I opened my mouth to speak, but Joy continued, her face very serious.

"I know you've told me not to take my bank down from my closet and not to play with money. But my friend wanted me to do it, and I just didn't want to tell her no!"

When I didn't answer, Joy added pensively, "It seems like when I'm with a friend, I'm always tempted to do what I know I'm not supposed to do."

"Why do you think you feel that way?"

"'Cause I want people to like me, and I'm afraid if I say no, they won't like me. But then I feel terrible! I knew I couldn't feel okay until I was with you again."

I took a deep breath. This was one of those God-designed situations I always hoped would come my way. Now I prayed that the Lord would make me sensitive to use this teachable moment to guide my precious child on the path of truth.

I opened Joy's Bible and showed her the verse in 1 John 1:9: "If we confess our sins, He is faithful and righteous to forgive us our sins and to cleanse us from all unrighteousness." For the next few minutes I explained again what sin is and why Christ had to come to pay the penalty for our sin. I shared with her my own desire to please people and told about a similar incident in Sarah's life and what negative consequences had ensued. I reminded her that "all have sinned and fall short of the glory of God" (Romans 3:23) but that God in his grace forgives us when we repent and turn back to him.

Though Joy had heard this explained to her many times, she was beginning to understand what this meant to her personally because of the awareness she had in her own heart of how easily she could be tempted to go against her conscience. I was glad to see she had a sensitive, responsive conscience, which is so valuable in our walk with the Lord. And I was especially grateful for the chance to model God's grace for her.

"Joy," I said, "I think we need to pray together to God. I would like you to tell him what you did that was wrong. That's what confession means. Then let's thank him that he loves you and will always forgive you for anything you ever do. Then I will pray and thank him too."

So we prayed. "Everything's okay now, right?" Joy said.

"Right."

"You're not mad at me?"

"No, I'm happy you did the right thing."

And Joy was happy too. "I think that's what it meant when Pilgrim had to get that burden off his back by laying it at the cross," she pronounced. "Remember when we read that in our *Dangerous Journey* book?[1] I just wanted you to help me get this burden off my back, Mom!"

The rest of the evening, Joy unloaded all sorts of dreams, desires, and confessions that burden the heart of a young girl. We talked and talked. We prayed together for God's forgiveness, and I hugged her and kissed her and told her I would always love her, "no matter what!" Finally we snuggled down under her covers and turned on the VCR.

She didn't even seem to notice that I dozed through most of the movie!

When it was over, she patted me on the head and stroked my hair as she had done since she had been a baby.

"Mommy, I feel so close and secure when I get to be with you like this! I like my friends, but I needed time alone with you so you could help me not feel guilty and tell me again about how to be with my friends. Thanks for being close to me, Mom! I just like to be *with* you!"

Though I desire my children to live righteously and to avoid doing things they know are wrong, I know that they, like me, will fall short of their own and Christ's standards. I am so thankful Joy feels she can come to me when she has done something wrong. By guiding her to the throne of God, I become like Christ to her as she develops her understanding of how to deal with the reality of sin and guilt. I give her the same gift of grace that has been so crucial in my own life.

After all, though I desire to live righteously and perfectly for the Lord, I know I will never be able to live up perfectly to his standards or even to mine. That is why the grace of God has meant so much to me. I know I will fail, but I also know he is faithful and just to forgive *my* sin and cleanse me of all my unrighteousness.

Beyond that, though, I have learned that maturity in Christ is not instantaneous but a slow process. Even as a real human being starts off as a baby and matures toward adulthood, making mistakes and learning along the way, so Christian believers—including my children—start out immature and move gradually toward maturity. It is gracious forgiveness that enables us all to move past our mistakes and keep on growing. Even more important, it is forgiving grace that makes real love possible in our lives.

Luke 7:36-50 tells us of a time when one of the Pharisees actually invited Jesus to dine with him. I like to think he was still grasping for the true meaning of spirituality and desired in his heart to know the true God. But he failed miserably because he missed the whole point of grace.

During this dinner a woman in the city who had a reputation as a sinner sought Jesus out. She actually came into the Pharisee's home, and she stood behind Jesus weeping, her heart surely broken and contrite from years of guilt and pain. In an outpouring of love, the broken woman began to wet Jesus' feet with her tears and then anointed his feet with perfume from an alabaster vial, obviously a precious treasure to her. This act of worship was from her heart, an expression of deep appreciation that Jesus had loved her and forgiven her.

This "sinner" woman clearly understood what grace was about, but

Jesus' Pharisee host didn't have a clue. His heart was too full of judgment to see his own need. "If this man were a prophet," he thought, "He would know who and what sort of person this woman is who is touching Him, that she is a sinner" (7:39).

How interesting it is to see that Jesus knew what the man was thinking. He then told the man a story about two debtors who owed a great deal of money. Both were forgiven of their debts. Jesus then asked the Pharisee, "Which person will love the moneylender more?"

"I suppose the one whom he forgave more," was his reply.

Jesus then reminded his host, the Pharisee, that he had not even washed Jesus' feet when he entered the home. But the woman had not ceased to wash his feet and kiss them. "For this reason I say to you, her sins, *which are many,* have been forgiven, for she loved much; but he who is forgiven little, loves little."

This is an important word to us as parents. Sometimes we feel that we need to play the role of the Holy Spirit in our children's lives and impose great guilt on them so they will be hesitant to sin anymore. But I don't see this in the life of Jesus. Yes, Jesus always called his disciples and followers to the highest standards. He taught that he came to fulfill the law and that all the commandments of God were of utmost importance (Matthew 5:17-20). And yet, wherever he went, Jesus proclaimed forgiveness and extended his gracious forgiveness to all who sought him—including tax collectors, prostitutes, and even a thief on the cross. He maintained this same attitude of gentle and gracious forgiveness toward the disciples even as they abandoned him at the cross. Jesus took the time to personally talk to them about sin and to offer them grace. And it was this gracious forgiveness, I believe, that opened their hearts so that they "loved much."

Our children need the same kind of gentle graciousness from us if they are to learn to share their vulnerability, to confess their own sin, and to be free to love. If they fear our strong condemnation and possible rejection, they will hide their sin, perhaps even deceive themselves about the nature of it. They will definitely not avail themselves of our mature direction in their lives.

The very essence of God's grace, his unmerited favor in our lives, is the initiation of his love and grace toward us when we weren't even aware of our need. Romans 5:8 tells us that "God demonstrates His own love toward us, in that while we were yet sinners, Christ died for us." Because our children inherited our sinful nature, they are by nature separated from God. Yet Christ came into the world as a humble and generous redeemer, offering his unlimited forgiveness and redemption to all who would come to him.

I believe we must strive to model that kind of gracious, forgiving love to our children. Of course we must instruct them in righteousness so they will understand the law of righteousness that is written in their hearts (Romans 1:18-19). We must teach them what sin is, and we must discipline them appropriately when they knowingly stray. Yet we must also show them, as Christ did for his disciples, what it means to be able to go to the throne of God to receive forgiveness, the cleansing of our hearts, and God's unconditional love. And we must do this not only by talking about God's love (and being honest about our own need for forgiveness), but by making sure our children experience unconditional love and acceptance from us.

Extending grace to our children not only gives them a living picture of God's love, it also lays for them a foundation for healthy relationships. The two greatest commandments, remember, are summed up by Jesus as loving God and loving people (Matthew 22:37-40). As we seek to pass on a picture of God's grace to our children and model his gracious gift of love and forgiveness to all people, we help our children obey both commandments. We teach them to love God, and we give them the desire and ability to extend grace to others. In the process, we help them develop intimate relational skills and give them a head start for mature, productive relationships—in family, friendship, marriage, ministry, and work.

Giving our children this gift of forgiving grace can transform their lives by helping them understand that a relationship with God is not something that can be earned by good behavior but a free gift to be accepted with gratitude and repentance. This gift of grace will be with them forever in their lives. What a legacy of freedom, peace, and love to extend to our children—a legacy that will accompany them even into eternity.

–A Mother's Prayer–

Precious Redeemer,
Thank you for the compassionate grace you showed in redeeming us
and dying for us when we were yet sinners. Help us to visualize our-
selves as extensions of your forgiving and redeeming grace to our chil-
dren. Please help them learn how to give grace at home so that they
might do the same for the people you bring into their lives.

Amen

For Study and Discussion

Giving Your Children the Gift of Grace

1. Read Romans 2:4. According to this verse, what leads us to repent? How specifically does God want you to extend his grace to your children so that his kindness, through you, will lead them to repentance?

2. Read Mark 14:66-72 and then 1 Peter 4:8. Knowing that Christ gave Peter grace after he failed so miserably, how would he have you extend this kind of grace to your own children? What would this look like in your daily interactions?

3. The last night Jesus had with his disciples, he called them "little children" (John 13:33). Does this tell you anything about his attitude toward these grown men who were his most devoted followers? Read John 14:1 and see what his continued response was to Peter after he had confronted him with the fact that he would deny Christ. How does this show the loving grace that Jesus extended to his disciples? How does he want you to extend it to your children?

4. The Bible makes it clear that we are to discipline and correct our children when they do wrong. How do you do this faithfully while still giving them the gift of grace?

5. Write down what tends to irritate you about each of your children

and sometimes keeps you from showing God's gracious love. Pray for each child he has given into your hands and make a plan for how you will respond more graciously to him or her, especially in those irritating situations.

PART TWO

The Gift of Inspiration

From the very beginning, God created men and women to be like him and to fellowship with him. He also gave them a job to do: "subduing the earth" and making it flourish in every area from government to medicine, music to literature, finances to farming. He provided human beings with a wide scope of opportunities in which to glorify God and to share in his creative nature.

After the fall of man, restoring the world to God's purposes and promoting the messages of the kingdom of God became a part of the great work God intended to share with his followers. Imparting this great purpose to our children will appeal to the design of God written into their hearts. They are made to respond to God's call in their lives. We give them the gift of inspiration when we help them heed that call.

Inspiration leads us to follow
God's purposes.

Chapter 5

On the Mountain—a Model for Inspiration

The well-traveled road was bathed in late afternoon sunlight at the end of a warm day. There were small groups of merchants returning from Jericho, families nearing the end of their journey back home after a trip to Jerusalem, and market vendors transporting their wares. Small carts packed to bursting with crates of cooing doves, barrels of fragrant olive oil, and caskets of salted fish took up much of the roadway, forcing the huddled groups of pedestrians to move aside to make room.

The crowded road, marked deeply with rutted tracks, was filled with the constant hum of busyness and noise, and for the small group on their way to Bethany, keeping up with each other was quite a task. The men and women made a motley crew, but the air around them was charged with excitement, energy, friendliness, and, most of all, anticipation. The men known as Jesus' disciples stuck close together, each wanting to catch every

word of conversation as they moved closer to the meeting place on Mount
Olivet, where they would once again speak with their beloved Master. Jesus
himself had picked the place, and the expectation was high as they pondered just what the meeting would hold.

Jesus had always loved the cool, windblown summit of Olivet, where a
cluster of twisted, old olive trees provided an oasis of shade in a comfortable, tangled garden. So many times they had lounged together there, fresh
breezes wafting over them as they gazed down on the gleaming white
buildings of Jerusalem. The secluded place provided a welcome escape
from the bustle that filled almost every moment of Jesus' days, a reprieve
from the crowds of people who needed so much of him, and the night sky
over Olivet had provided a wide-open canopy of space where he could pray
undistracted. The disciples remembered so many days and nights there, so
many wonderful, from-the-heart conversations. They had learned so much
from Jesus there on the mountain.

To the disciples, each bend of the familiar road seemed crowded with
specific memories of time spent with their Lord. Hadn't he gone to the
mountain on the morning of the day when the adulterous woman was
thrown on the ground and accused before him in the temple? Maybe the
Father had spoken to him in advance of what would happen. And this was
the very mountain where all the people had spread out garments and leafy
branches on this very road and pronounced him as the one who "came in
the name of the Lord." He had been cresting the hill on this road when he
caught sight of the city and wept that it had so long rejected the Father.
Here he had told them that if they had faith, they could actually move the
mountain—now *that* was an idea! And he had described the destruction of
Jerusalem and the end of the world while they sat together in the protec-

tive shade of the trees. And in a garden nearby, six weeks earlier, Judas had betrayed him as he was praying.

Since then so much had happened, so much that was baffling and terrifying and exhilarating, and these events filled the travelers' conversations as well. Jesus had been framed by the Pharisees, put to death by the Romans, and then—astoundingly—he had risen again. They had all seen him in the past forty days—had spoken with him, touched him, broken bread with him. He had showed himself to a weary pair on the road to Emmaus, appeared in a closed upper room to the disciples, even cooked breakfast on the shore of Galilee. It was as if he delighted in surprising them with his companionship, giving them a visual remembrance that he would always be with them—personally with them—as they went about their lives.

As the men and women neared the end of their journey, the conversations quieted, and their heartbeats quickened. What important message might the Master have for them today?

A small group of people had already gathered at the summit, each pair of eyes searching expectantly for one important Person. Suddenly a hush fell upon the crowd. Everyone's face seemed drawn toward the east, where a deep blue sky sparkled between the lacy olive branches. And there, at last, was the shining, laughing, familiar face of the Lord Jesus. His radiant eyes filled with light and life as he looked out lovingly through the crowd, welcoming familiar friends and holding up his hands to greet and bless them. His presence was as familiar as that of a friend, yet he had the command and dignity of royalty holding court.

One man yelled out, "Lord, is it at this time you are restoring the kingdom to Israel?" An excited murmur of interest spread among the crowd at this possibility. But Jesus rose to his fullest stature and commanded the attention of all who were present with the resounding voice of authority.

"It is not for you to know times or epochs which the Father has fixed by his own authority."

A buzz of conversation ran through the crowd at this response, and some exchanged doubtful glances as Jesus continued, "But you will receive power when the Holy Spirit has come upon you; and you shall be my witnesses both in Jerusalem, and in all Judea and Samaria, and even to the remotest part of the earth."

At this the crowd fell silent again. Jesus barely had to raise his voice to be heard as he challenged them to "make disciples of all the nations... teaching them to observe all that I commanded you." And then he concluded with a loving reassurance: "I am with you always, even to the end of the age."

The words seemed to burn in the hearts of his followers as they finally began to understand the significance of their own lives. This is why they were here, what they had been born for! The Master had chosen each of them specially—fishermen, tax collectors, prostitutes, children, men and women of no special background—to be the "sent" ones, the Lord's ambassadors to the whole world.

Now so much of what Jesus had said before finally made sense. So that's what he had meant when he called his disciples at the beginning of his ministry and mysteriously told them, "I will make you fishers of men!" And that was the reason for that memorable prayer in the Upper Room, almost his last words to them before proceeding to the Garden of Gethsemane: "As you sent me into the world," he had prayed, "I also have sent them into the world." How amazing that he would share the glory of himself and his Father and his kingdom through the lives of such ordinary people, that they would be allowed to be part of this world-changing work!

They were still trying to take it all in when a billowing cloud rolled down from the sky. With outstretched arms seeming to simultaneously embrace and bless those present in the crowd, Jesus began to rise upward toward the ethereal cloud.

Jaws dropped. Every eye turned skyward. And then, after an instant of glory, Jesus was gone. The crowd was left staring open-mouthed into the air.

Suddenly two men in white clothing were standing before them. In voices strong with the glory of heaven, they cried, "Men of Galilee, why do you stand looking into the sky? This Jesus, who has been taken up from you into heaven, will come in just the same way as you have watched him go."[1]

What a wonderful experience it would have been to behold the spectacular ascension of Jesus into heaven. Just as God announced Jesus' birthday with a host of singing angels, so he marked his "heaven going" with a flourish of cloud and still more angels. These particular angels, who promised that Jesus would return, gave a surge of hope to all who followed him—a hope so strong that his return is mentioned more than three hundred times in the New Testament.

It's especially interesting to me to realize that three gospel accounts and the book of Acts record Jesus' last instructions to go into all the world. This very fact underlines the importance these instructions held in the minds of his first followers, those who would eventually record the story of his life. Not only had Jesus come into the world to redeem it for the sake of his Father, he had also come to train leaders who would continue the Father's redeeming work. As Jesus was sent into the world, so are we, and so are our children.

As mothers and fathers, it is so easy to get distracted by the details of our lives. We have so much to do! We must feed our children well and take care of their health. We must oversee their education and their training to make sure they will be able to take care of themselves and live in a civilized society. We train them in righteousness so they may understand how God wants them to live. We try to relate to them in mature ways and help them learn to have healthy relationships.

Yet often, I think, we get lost in these multitudinous tasks that rule our lives, and we lose sight of the underlying purpose behind all these tasks, which is to prepare our children to go into the world and make disciples for our Lord.

Jesus promised that he would be with us. He also promised that he will come back. It is to him that we will have to give an account of how faithfully we sought to pass on his message and his commission to our children. Giving our children the gift of inspiration—helping them understand their spiritual purpose, which is to glorify God and to make him known—is one of the most crucial tasks of Christian parenting.

From the time the first man and woman turned away from him, God has sought to redeem us back to himself. His plan for accomplishing this task has been to use real people, made in his likeness. Jesus, of course, was the culmination of that plan—God's actual presence in human form. But since then each of us, including our children, has a part to play in that ongoing story of redemption.

Each of our children has been given a specific personality and a particular set of circumstances that will give shape to God's purpose for his or her life. It is our privilege and responsibility as parents to help our children understand their particular fit in God's plan. This means pointing out special skills and talents. It also means helping children realize that God didn't give them such skills and talents just to use on themselves, but to glorify him and bring others to him through the stewardship of their lives. In other words, we are to help them see themselves and their potential and then to inspire them for God's purposes:

"Joel, you are so musical. Maybe you will write great music that will encourage others to worship God and to want to know him!"

"Nathan, you are so friendly and outgoing, I know God will use your personality and skills as a magician to reach out to many and to make a bridge for them to understand the gospel."

"Sarah, what an excellent writer you are. You are also so artistic. I'm eager to see how God can use your work to encourage others to understand him better or to appreciate the beauty and design of his creation!"

"Joy, you are so compassionate. I love the sweet cards you make! I can see the Lord using you to comfort and encourage many lonely or hurting people."

As mothers, we have the hearts and the trust of our children from the earliest moments of their lives, and they need us for so many reasons. They naturally look to us for physical sustenance, protection, affection. Deep in their hearts, however, they also long for a special place to belong, a place to feel their worth, and they need us to help them find it. These precious children were designed to fulfill a purpose for God by bringing his glory to bear through their lives. They were designed to be his hands, his voice, his heart and mind through the various kinds of work they undertake in his world.

When we remind our children of their eternal significance, using everything from lullabies to bedtime stories to simple phrases such as "I wonder how God will use you in the world?" we help fulfill the deepest need of their hearts to be a part of a kingdom that is much greater than they have ever seen or known. As we seek to give our children the gift of inspiration, we will find ourselves being pulled down the road of our own purpose and significance, and we will intuitively verify the importance of God's design for motherhood.

Chapter 6

Inspiring a Sense
of Purpose

As an introverted dreamer type of personality, I require some alone time just to gain equilibrium for daily tasks. This need has driven me to develop the habit of getting up between half past four and half past five in the morning so I can have time to myself to think, pray, sit, read, and prepare for what the day will bring. Any other time of the day, our highly active crew of six people is awake and wandering around somewhere, and there's no way to find the total peace and quiet I crave.

On one particular morning, as I reflected on the needs of my family and the demands of the coming week, the Lord put Joel on my heart. At sixteen, my six-foot-three, gentle-spirited son is a mixture of mystery and promise. His quiet nature provides a soothing touch to our family rambunctiousness, but it also makes him harder to know. I've learned I need to seek him out alone if I'm to know what's going on inside. I've realized over the years that Joel is a lot like me—pondering many things in his heart that aren't always obvious to the louder, more active types surrounding him.

As I sat there praying for Joel and his future and his needs and desires, I suddenly had a thought: *I'll wake him up and sneak him out to breakfast so we can talk and I can see what is on his heart.*

Joel was all for it once I managed to wake him up. Individual attention can be hard to come by in the group atmosphere. He quickly rolled out of bed and hurried out to the car.

Just a month before, Clay and I had taken Joel for some career testing that evaluated his aptitudes, skills, and strengths. The test took into account desires and personality as well as abilities and was supposed to be useful in giving direction for further education and training. The man evaluating the test assertively explained Joel's test results and went into detail about what areas he thought would be best for him to pursue as a possible career. Clay, Joel, and I had fun on the way home talking about what the test had revealed. We were all surprised about the number of career possibilities the testing agent had suggested that we had never considered. For the moment we were all in agreement with the test's assessment.

As the days went by, however, I had felt a nagging struggle develop in my heart about some of what the man had said to Joel. I couldn't put my finger on what was bothering me though. I thought perhaps we could talk about it over breakfast.

After our hunger was satisfied with a Cracker Barrel feast of scrambled eggs, toast, biscuits, grits, and bacon, we both relaxed with a mug of hot coffee and settled in for the important, secret-sharing talk that usually took place at our private meetings. Having satiated his manly appetite, Joel was ready to plunge in. I asked him what he had been thinking about during the weeks after the test and if he agreed with the assessment he had been given.

"You know, Mom, the test told me a lot that I already knew, and *that* built some confidence in my mind. It was good to know I really am gifted in some of the areas I have always enjoyed—you know, like playing music or designing and structuring things."

I laughed. "You mean like 'organizing lists of facts and assimilating data' and 'working best in the context of accountability with a team of people'?"

He laughed too, remembering the assessor's professional jargon. "Yeah," he said. "Stuff like that can make a normal personality sound important. And it makes sense what he said—that maybe I'd do well as an architect or a graphic designer. But you know, in the past few days I think I've realized something that's more important than any of the things he told me."

My heart stirred when he said that. So Joel, too, had been bothered a little by that visit. I couldn't wait to hear what insight he had come to.

"The man who tested me is a nice pagan," Joel went on. "He's developed lots of skills at testing people in the areas of secular work. But he isn't a believer. He isn't committed to having a ministry to others. He doesn't have an eternal perspective on the importance of answering to God for our time and skills. So his world-view just doesn't provide for the same goals I have developed."

I sat there amazed as Joel talked, amazed to hear such mature eloquence coming from the mouth of my sixteen-year-old. "Mom, he never even mentioned any options in full-time Christian work," Joel went on. "And I think that's what I want to do. I've realized through all of this that I really want to be in ministry, to serve God with my whole life. That's the kind of 'career answer' I'm looking for—to figure out what God wants me to do with all the skills and strengths he has given me. So I've been looking on the Internet at colleges that have missions and ministry as a major or minor. I've found several places where I can get the training I need to go full time into some sort of ministry. Do you think I'm thinking right, Mom?"

It was one of those parenting moments when the Lord's presence seems to fill my heart with his assuring companionship and voice of encouragement: *See, he really was listening all those years when you were seeking to reach his heart for my purposes. I have been working through it all to reach down into his heart and call him to myself. He has made the choice to follow. You can trust me to continue the work I have started!*

Jesus' work in a person's life has always begun with a call to leave behind the goals, purposes, and distractions of this world and to say yes to a whole new life, a new way of thinking. "Follow me" is what he told the disciples as he recruited them. And they did, abandoning their fishing nets, their tax-collector's moneybags, their permanent homes, their everyday duties and pleasures. And they never went back. Sure, they still did a little fishing from time to time! But once they made the choice to follow Jesus, their lives were forever changed. They never returned to "normal."

I think this is vital for us to keep in mind as Christians and as parents. We know we are called to follow Christ, to take his message to the world, to raise our children to heed Jesus' call. But sometimes I think we fail to consider that following the Lord might mean leaving behind the ordinary and the familiar. It means exchanging a temporal view of life for an eternal goal. And this may mean leaving behind things we really care about—involvements and pursuits that seem important and worthwhile but may not be God's best for us.

Part of giving the gift of inspiration is helping our children understand this—and perhaps reminding ourselves. To fulfill God's design for their lives, our precious children must at some point determine to give Jesus allegiance in every aspect of their lives. There is a cost to discipleship, and that cost is everything!

In Luke 14:25-35, Jesus addresses some of these issues. Verses 27-31 are poignant to anyone considering the cost of following God's purposes:

> Whoever does not carry his own cross and come after Me cannot be My disciple. For which one of you, when he wants to build a tower, does not first sit down and calculate the cost to see if he has enough to complete it? Otherwise, when he has laid a foundation and is not able to finish, all who observe it begin to ridicule him, saying, "This man began to build and was not able to finish." Or what king, when he sets out to meet another king in battle, will not first sit down and consider whether he is strong enough with ten thousand men to encounter the one coming against him with twenty thousand?

Jesus sums up his talk to his disciples by saying, "So then, none of you can be My disciple who does not give up all his own possessions."

In Matthew 10:39, Jesus put it even more graphically: "He who has found his life will lose it, and he who has lost his life for My sake will find it." And even earlier in Matthew (6:19-21,24), Jesus cut to the heart of our service to himself:

> Do not store up for yourselves treasures upon earth, where moth and rust destroy, and where thieves break in and steal. But store up for yourselves treasures in heaven, where neither moth nor rust destroys, and where thieves do not break in or steal; for where your treasure is, there your heart will be also.... No one

can serve two masters; for either he will hate the one and love
the other, or he will be devoted to one and despise the other.
You cannot serve God and wealth.

Jesus is absolutely clear about the kind of choices we all must make to
follow him. And that itself is out of the ordinary when you think about it.
The choice is ours! Jesus calls us to follow, but he doesn't demand. He *beck-
ons* us to follow, to live for his purposes.

It might seem to us that a perfectly powerful God should be able just
to use his authority to force all people to believe in him. Or perhaps he
could perform a sign in the sky and miraculously attract all of us to his
power and glory. Couldn't he use media to manifest himself all over the
world at the same time so that all of us could hear his voice and come to
know him at the same time?

Recently, during the Christmas season, I often heard a song on the
radio by the music group 4HIM. The song describes the way God reached
down from heaven and chose a simple carpenter and a peasant girl to be
the earthly parents of his child, Jesus, the Savior of the whole world. The
line that caught my attention each time says, in essence, that's a pretty
strange way to redeem the world.

Indeed it seems strange to us that Jesus would choose to use sinful, fallible people to share his glory and to manifest his kingdom to the world.
How interesting that he would use simple fishermen, unsavory types like
tax collectors, and "second-class" women to be those who heard his words,
saw his miracles, and were asked to spread his kingdom to the ends of the
earth.

But that's exactly the point. The Lord's ways are not our ways. His
kingdom comes in ways we would never expect. And he wants us to know

that when we choose to follow him, our lives will never again follow familiar, ordinary paths.

If I seek to inspire my children to understand and own God's purposes for their lives, that means they will grow up with a different set of instructions than people in the world have. Not only will their values be different, but their ideas of "what I want to be" should be different as well. The Lord will require each of us who know him and understand his message of salvation in our own lives to be good stewards of that message as long as we live on this earth. I'm sure he will ask us, "What did you do to make me known to the people I brought into your life?"

Does that mean that, as a Christian, Joel could not in good conscience be an architect or an ordinary musician—that he couldn't serve God without going into full-time ministry? Of course not. Many Christians make a huge impact for Christ from the platform of regular secular jobs.

What really mattered in Joel's case was not his decision but his questions. Instead of asking, "What kind of job should I train for?" or "What kind of career do I want?" he was asking, "With all the skills, background, and personality the Lord has given me, how can I best serve him and tell others about his kingdom? What job should I pursue so that I may serve him best in all that I do?"

That kind of question is at the heart of what it means to follow Christ. It's the way we all must learn to think as disciples, and it's what we must try to instill in our children through our words and our examples. We must strive as a family to keep our focus on the eternal, not the ordinary. We must be willing to pay the cost of discipleship, determined to lay up our treasures in heaven.

When we do this, our children will have the freedom and peace to know that God is not measuring them by how much money they make, what kind of car they drive, or how big a house they are able to buy. By God's standards, our children will be successful in life if they are willing to love and follow Christ wherever they are asked to go. And that is an attainable goal. What he has called us to do he will give us the ability to complete.

That is a final important word to me as a mother committed to discipling my children. I can train. I can teach. I can strive to be an example and to give my children the gift of inspiration. But it is Jesus who calls them, just as he calls me. And they, in the end, are the ones who must make the choice to follow him into extraordinary life.

I am so thankful to Joel for reminding me that God is at work in his heart to cultivate all that had been planted there. How reassuring to know that, though I had sought to teach Christ's purposes, the Lord Jesus would be the one to complete the work. After all, he is the one in charge of my children.

But what a privilege it is to have been included in bringing about this miracle of calling. What a great idea God had to use mothers as a part of that process—of helping to inspire our children to God's purposes and walking alongside them as they learn to make the choice of leaving the world.

—A MOTHER'S PRAYER—

Ever-Living Lord,
Help us understand how brief our lives on earth are in comparison to
eternity with you. Help us not to get so caught up in mundane par-

enting issues that we forget to focus our children's hearts on your kingdom. Above all, give our children a passion for you and your purposes. Build a heritage of righteousness in the lives of our children so that generations to come may serve you faithfully.

Amen

Chapter 7

Inspiring a Sense of God's Powerful Presence

Mondays in the Clarkson home usually find all of us trying to recover and adjust from the weekend—those glorious hours of sleeping late, enjoying endless cups of tea and hot chocolate, talking together over casual, long-drawn-out meals, reading magazines or books, watching favorite movies, playing rowdily in the yard with friends, and riding bikes or exploring. We return reluctantly to the realm of responsibility in which all the messes of Saturdays and Sundays must be dealt with and the duties of Monday through Friday attended to with full force.

This particular Monday was no exception. Orphan cups and mugs, discarded baskets of popcorn, and untold numbers of socks had to be picked up from the various places they had been dropped. Individual breakfasts were hurriedly prepared and wolfed down. Laundry baskets were ransacked for presentable shirts. Backpacks were loaded with assignments and pencils, and each person hurried off to his or her own place of work. Sarah, the most experienced of our teen drivers, was recruited to take the two youngest to some Monday morning classes. When she came home, she hurried to her desk and tried to get started on her own work. But even with the younger children gone, the interruptions didn't stop. Sarah was really getting frustrated.

After graduating from high school, Sarah had decided to delay college for a year or two. She had already published one book, and she wanted to see if she could get another one under her belt before plunging into the rigors of higher education. But this meant she was home, and being the eldest child in a large family almost inevitably means getting caught up in family responsibilities and duties. Our move added to the amount of work to be done, because our regular support systems were not yet in place. So Sarah had done more than her share of helping with laundry, dishes, cooking, reading to the younger kids, and answering the phone. Usually she did it with good cheer, but I was aware of her frustration. And Mondays, especially, seemed to do her in.

"Mom, what I really need is a patron," Sarah signed in frustration when she came to the kitchen for a drink of water. "I need someone who will pay me to live somewhere very private and beautiful so that I won't have to spend so much time on daily, routine tasks! Then I could just sit around thinking great thoughts that would turn into great books!"

"Oh, honey, if you just knew how many times I've had those thoughts!" was my sympathetic reply. "But what I really want is a full-time maid!"

And so went the day, with more chores, more interruptions, more responsibilities, more frustrations. Then about five o'clock on that crisp autumn afternoon, just as I was finishing an e-mail on my computer and getting ready to start dinner, I looked out my window and caught my breath.

"Sarah, quick!" I called out as I ran to the front door to grab my jacket. "Come look!"

She dropped what she was doing and got her jacket too. Together we hurried down the street toward the cow field that backed up to our property. We quickly scaled the fence and ran out into the field.

Before us was one of the most beautiful sights I ever remember seeing. The entire skyline was lit as though on fire. Crimsons and corals and pinks painted the sky in brilliant, spectacular hues. The range of tall trees in the line of the setting sun seemed to flame and sparkle in the shifting light. A cold, soft breeze blew gently on our faces and in our hair to remind us it wasn't a real fire we were watching but the result of God's masterful artistry.

We stood in silence for a few minutes, taking in the splendid sight that surrounded us. Everything in sight seemed to dance with fiery colors—the skies and trees, the horizon and clouds above. Then slowly, slowly the colors began to fade. We stood there and marveled until we were standing together in darkness.

"Oh, Mama!" Sarah exclaimed, using her affectionate name for me. "That was spectacular! How could anyone see something like that and not believe in God?"

We walked home quietly, our souls filled with the warmth and grandeur one feels when she has seen the fingertips of God. More important, we were at peace—no longer caught up in the irritating, mundane world but soothed by that God-given reminder of the Lord's power and presence.

When I first became a mother, I would never have guessed that the words *Come, look!* would be so important to my children's faith training. But as we all grew together, I came to understand the importance of pointing out to them the abundant evidence of God's power and glory and presence that surrounds us. This act of directing their eyes and ears beyond the mundane to the wonders of God's work is one of the most important ways I can give my children the gift of inspiration.

God is more powerful, mysterious, and wonderful than we can ever imagine. He cannot be contained by our thoughts or definitions and is in a sense wild and untamable and bigger than we are in every way. And yet he is also a God who goes to great lengths to reveal himself to us, to remind us that he is present in all the minutes of our lives. If we have eyes to see and ears to hear, the evidence of his power and presence is all around us. And those moments when we see him revealed teaches us so much. Even in the darkest moments of our own small lives, he gives us reason to trust him, to anticipate the miraculous, to dream of resurrection life and the hope it brings.

It's so easy for our human spirits to get bogged down in the tangible realities of each day—a flat tire on a car, a child's croupy cough in the middle of the night, another bill to pay when our bank account is already overdrawn, another round of bickering with brothers or sisters. Jesus' disciples also found themselves weighted down on a daily basis. Often it was only at the Lord's prompting that they stopped to look beyond their mundane responsibilities and to remember that so much more was going on in their lives than traveling dusty roads and taking care of speaking arrangements and crowd control.

Jesus often made use of the world around him to confront his followers with the reality of his supernatural existence, to point them beyond predictable circumstances and enlarge their narrow vision. Sometimes he called attention to supernatural reality by means of a miracle. He healed the sick (Mark 1:34). He turned the tide of fishing expeditions (Luke 5:4-7; John 21:5-6), calmed storms (Matthew 8:23-26), and walked on water (Matthew 14:23-31). At other times he pointed to natural reality—storms, floods, trees and their fruit, grapes and vines, flowers, birds, wind and waves—as evidence of the Father's work and his presence.

One of the places he did this most effectively was in the Sermon on the Mount, which is among my favorite passages of Scripture. Its truths can be studied and read and applied over and over again and have carried me through many difficult times in my life. When I take time to consider the setting in which Jesus gave this set of teachings to his followers, I understand even more of what he was trying to teach them.

Matthew 4:23–5:1 sets up the scene. Jesus had been traveling through the regions of Galilee teaching in synagogues, speaking to small and large groups, and healing many people. We read that large crowds followed him from many villages in Galilee, the Decapolis (or "ten cities"—a Greek-influenced area where there was a loose confederation of cities), Jerusalem, Judea, and beyond. Jesus must have been weary and spent from giving out so much to so many, and yet he obviously drew deeply from his reserves. He "went up on a mountain" as was his habit, invited his disciples to sit near him, and began to speak words that would change lives.

There is a gently sloping hillside on the northeast corner near the Sea of Galilee where some have speculated he preached this message. Or it might have been another mountain. But it must have been a beautiful natural setting with grass, trees, flowers, birds, and possibly the sea sparkling nearby. Jesus used the very hillside for teaching eternal truths. To the thousands of spiritually hungry and hurting people surrounding him, he used the flowers and birds to proclaim the mysteries of the kingdom of God:

> For this reason I say to you, do not be worried about your life, as
> to what you will eat or what you will drink; nor for your body,
> as to what you will put on. Is not life more than food, and the

body more than clothing? Look at the birds of the air, that they do not sow, nor reap nor gather into barns, and yet your heavenly Father feeds them. Are you not worth much more than they?... And why are you worried about clothing? Observe how the lilies of the field grow; they do not toil nor do they spin, yet I say to you that not even Solomon in all his glory clothed himself like one of these. But if God so clothes the grass of the field, which is alive today and tomorrow is thrown into the furnace, will He not much more clothe you? (Matthew 6:25-26,28-30)

Can you imagine listening to these words while resting on the grass and watching the gentle mountain breeze entice the wildflowers into a delicate dance on the meadow as chirping birds fly effortlessly from tree to tree? How could you help but feel the pressures of your daily troubles lift as you breathe the fresh air and hear the voice of Truth remind you to rest and trust?

Note that what Jesus was doing in this passage was very similar to what I did with Sarah the day of that amazing sunset. He was saying, "Come look!" at God's handiwork and then pointing beyond the handiwork to God himself.

"Look," Jesus told the crowds and his disciples that day. "Observe." Another translation says "consider." Jesus wanted his followers to pay attention to God's reality and presence in the world around them. He also wanted them to ponder and focus their attention *beyond* the natural to the God who wanted them to trust him. He was giving them the gift of inspiration!

If we desire to pass on that gift to our children, we will always be on the lookout for opportunities to tell them to "look" and "observe" and ponder. We must be ready to point them to signs of his living presence in our daily lives—and also to point beyond our circumstances to him who is beyond the limitations of this world. This awareness of divine reality helps open their hearts to God's will and pleasure at any moment and to lift them above the tedium of the mundane.

Walking with God without the moment-by-moment awareness of our companionship with a divine being becomes just a hard, taxing obligation. A child who does not have the opportunity to marvel at the bigness of God, the wonders of his creation, and the reality of his supernatural work will tend to measure the questions about "who God is" according to his or her finite, limited perspective.

Paul wrote in Romans 1:20, "Since the creation of the world His invisible attributes, His eternal power and divine nature, have been clearly seen, being understood through what has been made."

When we take the opportunity to expose our children to the glory of God displayed in a rainbow or powerful ocean waves or a star-studded night sky, we are helping them understand that there is a Being much bigger than themselves who created the universe and holds it together with his power. When we tell them about our answered prayers and those amazing "coincidences" that confirm God's presence in our lives, we help them realize that God is close and caring and active in our daily circumstances. When we explain the things we have been able to do in the Holy Spirit's power that we couldn't accomplish alone, we help them understand how God works and what he can accomplish through us. As we tell them "look" and "observe," we instill the hope that a supernatural Being more powerful than we can understand intervenes in time and space to help us and to interact with our lives.

This knowledge of God's mystery and omnipotence, his active presence, and his constant love helps us—and our children—learn to stand before him with soft, teachable hearts. When we are ready to receive the grace of his power and presence into each moment of our lives, we cannot help but look differently at all our daily activities. When we learn to look and listen and ponder, our everyday moments can be transformed by the knowledge of a God whose companionship brings joy, "wind to our wings," and the possibility of a miraculous touch at any moment.

And when we convey this vision of God's powerful presence to our children, we give them the gift of joy in each moment and the knowledge that even in the tedium of commonplace chores the Lord is looking out for us, ready to give his help and strength and presence. As we inspire our children to look for God's glory and purposes in their lives, we help them learn to expect the supernatural grace that is always available to us. Even as they learn to treasure God's presence in what is seen—the lilies and the sunsets and the embrace of those they love—they also learn to live by the conviction of things that are unseen (Hebrews 11:1)—to walk joyfully in the light of God's powerful and supernatural presence.

–A MOTHER'S PRAYER–

Creator God,
We praise you, Father, for the magnificent gift of your creation. Help us learn to find a quiet place in the midst of each day so that we may see the evidence of your fingertips. Teach us to lead our children to heaven's throne as we stop to observe the stars, the seasons, the birds, the storms, and all that you made. May we all learn to wonder at your greatness and worship you for your handiwork.

Amen

Chapter 8

Inspiring a New Kind of Love

Sarah was putting the last artistic touches on a Christmas package. Always attentive to detail, she had adorned her gift with wrapping fit for a queen. Delicate snowflake tissue paper lined the shipping box in which she placed the foil-wrapped gift, making sure the curled ribbon wasn't crushed.

Seven-year-old Joy sat licking a cinnamon candy stick as she watched Sarah finish her task.

"You must be sending that package to one of your best friends! It's so beautiful! I wish I would get a package like that in the mail from one of my friends!"

"No, Joy. Actually, I'm sending this to a girl I just recently met on one of my trips."

"Well, why are you taking so much time to make it so pretty, since you hardly even know her? I think you should send it to your best friend!"

87

Sarah sat down at the cluttered kitchen table to explain.

"The girl I'm sending this present to probably won't get any other presents from friends. She's had a lot of problems and has been rejected by a lot of people in her life. Her mom has been married to two different men, and she has been real sad and lonely moving from house to house. I thought I would try to brighten her life just a little bit by sending this. And I'm putting it in a pretty package because she needs to know she is loved even more than my best friends need to know it."

"I'm glad you're my sister, Sarah!" Joy said as she skipped away from the table, satisfied in her soul with the answer Sarah had given.

When we consider how to pass on the gift of inspiration to our children, we often think of taking them to church or getting them involved in a children's program or youth group, and those activities can be very positive. But even more important, I believe, is doing for them what Sarah was doing for Joy and what Jesus did for his disciples: helping them develop a heart for ministry by showing them what it means to reach out in love and compassion to others.

Too often, I think, we are tempted to view outreach mostly in terms of missionaries reaching unchurched people in faraway lands or perhaps an evangelistic crusade for thousands or an enthusiastic youth-group rally. But Jesus gave us a very different model of ministry when he took the time to reach out to people he encountered in the course of his everyday life. He happened to go by Simon Peter's home after a trip to the synagogue, and while there, he healed Peter's sick mother-in-law (Mark 1:29-31). He went to a friend's house and scandalized the Pharisees by drinking and eating with the people he met there—"tax collectors and sinners" (Luke 5:29-32). He commended a Roman soldier in front of a crowd of people for his great faith (Matthew 8:5-13). Wherever he walked, he encountered people in need, he had compassion on them, and he helped them.

Note that the very people Jesus chose as a focal point of his ministry weren't accepted in the temple courts of his day. The Pharisees rejected them as unworthy, either because they were outsiders in their society (such as Romans or Samaritans) or because they did not keep all of the myriad rules the temple leaders had imposed. Many of the people Jesus reached out to probably would have felt out of place in the temple.

It's easy to condemn the Pharisees' attitude, but don't we sometimes do the same thing? Aren't there certain people we find acceptable for ministry and others who seem too threatening to reach? Are we tempted to avoid those who look different from us, who dress differently or perhaps have "unacceptable" life habits like swearing, smoking, or drinking? Do we sometimes avoid reaching out to people simply because they make us uncomfortable?

I'm sure that at times I've been guilty of this kind of "selective ministry." But I try to work against it because I know what it's like to be on the other side, to be judged as the wrong "type" for God. Several years after I accepted Christ, for instance, I ran into the girl who first showed me the evangelistic booklet *The Four Spiritual Laws,* which God used to bring me to himself. "You know, Sally," she reminisced, "you just didn't seem the type of person who would be interested in Christianity. You were so different from all my other Christian friends, I wasn't even sure you were sincere. I knew you had a lot of friends and you were one of the 'cool' people, and it didn't seem like you would feel a need to know God!"

My jaw dropped when she said that. To me, the whole process of coming to Christ had been exciting and life changing. It had never occurred to me that I wasn't the "type" to be a Christian.

Later, when I moved overseas to work as a missionary in Eastern Europe, one of my fellow workers looked me over and said, "You just don't look like a missionary—too flashy. I predict you won't even last a year!"

Once again, apparently, I didn't fit the stereotypic "Christian" mold. But I *did* last. I loved being a missionary. And I try to keep that in mind when I'm making decisions about whom to approach for Christ. I hope I can learn to see people—and teach my children to see them—the way Jesus did.

Jesus, as far as I can tell, never related to people according to how well they fit into a particular group. Instead, he saw them through the lens of their needs, and he loved them.

The disciples tried to shoo away a group of children whose mothers wanted them to be blessed by Jesus. But Jesus looked past all the runny noses and sticky fingers to see the open, innocent hearts of the children and the hopeful love of the mother. "Let the children alone," he told the disciples, "and do not hinder them from coming to Me; for the kingdom of heaven belongs to such as these" (Matthew 19:14). Then he invited them up and blessed them. (Can't you just see the mothers standing behind the children, coaxing them to run up there and not be shy?)

When Jesus stopped by a well in Samaria and found a woman drawing water, he looked past her nationality and her gender and her reputation as a loose woman—all of which should have kept a good Jewish man from speaking to her—to see someone thirsty for respect and significance and meaning in her life. In a time when it was uncommon even to give a woman the time of day, he chose to discuss important matters with her, to offer her the "living water" of salvation, even to make her a message bearer to her entire village. To a woman whose whole life experience was rejection and failure, he gave a real second chance.

In the same way, when a well-dressed, very proper young man asked him a theological question, he looked beyond the man's obvious external success and spoke to his true heart need, which was to surrender all of himself to God. "If you wish to be complete," Jesus told him gently, "go and sell your possessions and give to the poor, and you will have treasure in heaven; and come, follow Me" (Matthew 19:21). The young man couldn't manage it—at least not at that moment. But I have often wondered if perhaps Jesus' incisive but obviously loving words took root in his heart and later brought him back to the Lord.

In all of these and other examples, Jesus showed a picture of a living God who has compassion on all those who have lost their way in the world, regardless of their external circumstances. He showed a willingness to reach out to the broken and needy. Matthew 9:36-38 reveals Jesus' loving heart toward the people he met: "He felt compassion for them, because they were distressed and dispirited like sheep without a shepherd. Then He said to His disciples, 'The harvest is plentiful, but the workers are few. Therefore beseech the Lord of the harvest to send out workers into His harvest.'"

"He felt compassion for them." That's so important. Passing on the gift of inspiration to our children is partly a matter of vision, which helps them understand that God wants to use them in this world to spread his kingdom. But vision alone is not enough. The vision defines the purposes of God, but compassion defines the heart of the vision. When we understand that God's love reaches into the dark and depraved corners of people's lives to bring healing and eternal life, then we will see people not for what they are but for *who* they are—people Christ loves and who need his redemption.

Trying to love people the way Jesus did can be intimidating. It can push us well beyond our comfort boundaries. Yet as we make this effort our children will learn what real love—and real ministry—is all about. The flame of inspiration may well be lit as our children observe our love in action—and begin to see the results in people's lives.

When our family first moved to the Colorado Springs area, we discovered a wonderful little restaurant that served a "proper" British tea, complete with scones and clotted cream. Since "teatime" is one of my favorite experiences, I frequented the little café often with my children in tow. Over a period of time, we befriended one of the waitresses who became dear to us. Each time we visited, we learned more about her life. And each time we returned home, the kids would have new excitement about praying for her.

"Mom, maybe we can have her to our house for tea and have a chance to be her friend and help her know the Lord."

The Lord did open up an opportunity for us to share a couple of our books with her, to talk about the Lord, and to become even closer to her before we moved away. And when we drove through the area recently on a trip, we stopped by the restaurant for a surprise visit. Our waitress friend threw up her arms in surprise when she spotted us coming in the door, and she treated all of us to lunch. Tears filled our eyes as she told us how much we had meant to her. I feel quite sure we will talk about our friend and pray for her for years to come.

So often in the context of our family routines the Lord has given us opportunities to reach out to others. It might be a checkout clerk at the store, a lonely neighbor, a nurse at the doctor's office, or a pesky neighbor child who hangs out at our house every day while his mother is at work. Wherever the Holy Spirit places us is exactly where he can extend this special love through us. As we are faithful to take these opportunities to minister, our children will gradually get the idea that God wants to use them, one person at a time, to change the world by reaching out to people who need his love.

Romans 5:8 tells us that "God demonstrates His own love toward us, in that while we were yet sinners, Christ died for us." It wasn't while we were praying for him to come or while we were being godly but while we were deeply involved in our particular brand of selfishness and sin that Christ saw our need, reached out toward us by coming to earth, and gave himself up to death for our benefit.

When we seek to inspire our children, we need to model for them this initiating principle. That means we put out our spiritual antennas, so to speak, wherever we go, looking for people in need. Then we take steps to reach out to them in some way, whether or not they are people we would normally feel comfortable with or people we think are good "prospects" for accepting Jesus. Even as Jesus died for us when we needed it, following him means befriending others who, like us, are in need of his grace. Then, once a relationship is formed or a friendship is started, we seek opportunities to share the truth of God's love and forgiveness as gently and attractively as we are able.

When our children were young and we were training them to do household chores, often we would come into our kitchen and find a pile of dirty dishes. (Those piles can still be found on occasion today!) When we asked our children why the unwashed dishes were still in the sink, they would say, "Well, no one asked me to wash dishes." To which we would reply, "When you are mature, you will not require us to stand over you to see that you get your work done. You will do it because you see the need yourself, and you will take the initiative with no one even asking you to do so."

It works that way in the Christian life, too. As we mature in our love for the Lord and come to know him better, we will often feel compelled to reach out to others simply because we see the need—and because Christ's kind of love has become a part of us. Second Corinthians 5:14 reminds us that "the love of Christ controls us"; an even better translation is "compels us." In other words, Christ's spirit inside us will drive us to share his love with others, and we will take the initiative to be agents of his redemption. We share the gift of inspiration with our children as they see us reaching out to others and as we involve them in these acts of outreach.

I have found that young children are usually less reserved than adults when it comes to wanting to share generously with others. They are generally not as given to racial or social prejudice as we are. Therefore, as we have prayed for God to use our family in the world, their innocent and giving love has sometimes pulled us into situations that have really stretched us. My children, for instance, love to think they can always bring someone in need to "our house…because our mom always helps people when they need it!" This is not always convenient, but it is almost always of God. As we sought to give our children the gift of inspiration, they often gave it to us as well!

When we follow in the footsteps of Jesus to reach out in love to those in need, we will ignite in our children the sense that they are worthy to consider themselves part of the solution in meeting people's needs. Patterns of ministry will naturally be caught as they learn from us and from Jesus a new and initiating love. In the process they will be inspired to give themselves in ministry, to become skilled and loving workers for his harvest fields.

~A MOTHER'S PRAYER~

Lord of Love,
Thank you for the privilege of serving you! Open our eyes that we
might see each person as you see him or her—not as a "type" but as
someone you love and as someone who needs you. As we learn to live
out the reality of your call on our lives to love and serve others, help
us establish a pattern for our children that they may also learn to
recognize need and reach out in love.

Amen

For Study and Discussion

Giving Your Children the Gift of Inspiration

1. For each child in your household, write out a list of characteristics (personality traits, skills, interests, etc.) that you believe God can use for his purposes.

2. Referring to the lists you just made, write a letter to each child expressing what you see in him or her and affirming that God has a special place for that child in his kingdom purposes. Whether you share the letter with your child now or save it for a future time depends on your circumstances. Don't forget to commit this list to the Lord in prayer and specifically ask him for help in inspiring that child to use his or her gifts to help bring about God's kingdom.

3. Read Matthew 6:33. This passage is clear about what our priorities should be, but priorities easily become skewed in the course of daily life. Consider the way you spend your time and your money. What does this say to your children about what is most important to you, and is this the message you want to send? In light of this verse, should a mother's children be her first priority?

4. Read Matthew 6:25-30 and Psalm 19:1. Then think of a time and place where you really felt the power and magnificence of God as

displayed in the work of his creation. In the coming few weeks, be on the alert for opportunities to look, observe, ponder—and point out God's wonders to your children. Set a goal of saying, "Come, look!" at least once a day.

5. Read Matthew 9:36. Can you think of some fears or prejudices in your life or your particular culture that might keep you or your children from seeing people as Jesus did? (What kinds of people do you tend to shy away from or find it hard to care about?) What might help you overcome these attitudes?

PART THREE

The Gift of Faith

In order to know God and to follow his purposes, we must know and understand his Word, which is the primary source of our knowledge of him and his ways. Understanding our world and all of history from a biblical point of view gives us a trustworthy foundation upon which to base our decisions and commitments. Embracing God's Word as truth and learning to act on what we believe is the practical application of learning to think about life the way God thinks.

Faith leads us to stake our lives on God's truth
as revealed in his Word.

Chapter 9

Enough for a Lifetime—
a Model for Faith

The room was dark with night shadows. They crept over the dirt floor and the wooden walls that smelled of musty age, and to the old man sitting in the corner it seemed they brought a chill with them. A single, dripping candle on a bare wooden table cast uncertain light over the sheet of yellow parchment and the trembling hands of the man who wrote upon it.

His name was John.

The beloved disciple of Jesus was an old man now with sparse gray hair, bent shoulders, and a face that bore the deep creases of time. But his eyes still held their old glow, and they were filled with the same warmth of love as when Jesus called him so many long years past.

The man worked feverishly, his gnarled hand moving over the page as quickly as the arthritis would allow, his lips moving silently with the words he wrote. For a moment he paused, lifting eyes that peered into the past, and he whispered to himself the words he was writing:

"The world is passing away...but the one who does the will of God lives forever."

The world *was* passing away—all the grief and pain, all the wrongs and injustice, all the limited sight of the finite earth, all passing away. And a good thing it was, John reflected. The older he grew, the more clearly he saw the world's flaws. Thank God this life wasn't true reality—just a short visit to a fallen place. But he had not always seen it quite like that.

A smile came to his lips as he remembered the zeal of his younger days, his impatience for the Master to do something big. He had wanted Jesus to bring the whole world, Romans and all, to its knees. He had wanted the Lord's kingdom to come right then, right there. Jesus had been so patient as he explained to the disciples over and over that his kingdom was of heaven, not of this earth. Scenes from the past flashed across John's mind like short rays of sunlight as he sat in the near darkness and remembered...

There was Jesus standing tall on the hill outside Galilee, the wind blowing his hair and carrying his words to the far fringes of the crowds. "Rejoice," he cried—and every man, woman, and child there felt the joy grow in their hearts—"if you are persecuted for me, for your reward in heaven is great!" Perplexed at these words, the people whispered in amazement to one another. A reward in heaven? What could the Lord be talking about? A future kingdom that would be theirs if only they would believe for a little while?

There was Jesus staring at the back of a young man as he walked away from true life, unable to relinquish his riches on earth for an unimaginable treasure in heaven. "Truly I say to you," Jesus had said quietly, "there is no one who has left house or brothers or sisters or mother or father or children or farms, for my sake and for the gospel's sake, but that he will receive a hundred times as much now in the present age…and in the age to come, eternal life."

And there was Jesus, his eyes bright, his voice gentle at the Passover supper as he shared one last night with his chosen twelve. John closed his eyes as he remembered; how dear the memory was to him. He had leaned against the Master's shoulder, watching his beloved face as Jesus told them so warmly, so passionately about the short time of this world. Trouble would be theirs in this world, he had told them, but this world was not their home. Their home was with God, and they were not to fear, for he had overcome the world. He was going there to prepare a special place for them. "I will come again and receive you to myself!" he had promised. To spend the whole glorious span of eternity with him—that would be their reward.

Jesus had prayed that very evening, "Father, I desire that they also, whom you have given me, be with me where I am, so that they may see my glory which you have given me, for you loved me before the foundation of the world."

John had known then that Jesus wanted them to be in heaven with him, where he had been even in the beginning with the Father, and he wanted them to see his glory there. What joy they looked forward to! John's heart grew warm with the thought of what awaited him. Soon, very soon…

Tears filling his eyes, John was brought back to the present and its dark reality: a prison cell, the shadows, a body that ached with age and rough treatment, a heart that throbbed with loneliness and sorrow. Bleak was life to his eyes. But he did not despair. The tears were tears of joy, not sadness, for one more scene was playing before the eyes of his heart.

There once more was Jesus, standing in golden sunlight on a green hill, the wind dancing around him, his people gathered at his feet, their eyes on the light of his face. "Go," he had just told them, "tell the whole world of my love. And I will be with you always, always!" Then, oh then, a sudden glory of light had surrounded the Master. The clouds had parted and gathered around him as he began to rise into the air. The heavens had opened to receive the Son of God, and the people bound to earth had rejoiced to see their Savior in his true form. Many had wept as well, for as he went, the promise, the assurance of their future life with him was set in their hearts. Someday they, too, would rise to the arms of God and to life eternal.

John had remembered that day and that promise many times over the years. He'd recalled it as his feet marched weary roads, as the sting of a whip cut his back, as he sat in utter loneliness in a prison cell. He had described that day on the hill to every follower of Christ he met. He had turned it over in his mind and stamped it on his heart so he would never forget.

Now, huddled against the cold, John picked up his pen again. His body was chilled, but his eyes sparkled with excitement as he set to writing once more. His stiff fingers scratched against the paper for a while, and then he put the pen down. Holding up the paper, he read the last words out loud:

"This is the promise which he himself made to us: eternal life."

Unending, perfect, fulfilled life. No pain, no death, no wrongness, no evil, just an eternity spent in the company of Love himself. The kingdoms of the world would pass away, but the kingdom of heaven would never end.

And that was a promise worth waiting for.[1]

More than 180 times in the Gospels, Jesus spoke of the kingdom of God. He told of the comfort to be found there, he spoke of the King who rules there, he promised rewards for faithfulness that would be given there, and he painted pictures in people's minds of the mansions that were built there, waiting to be inhabited by his followers. He also emphasized again and again that God's kingdom operates on completely different principles from those our earthbound minds understand.

As we teach our children and lay a foundation of truth that will hold strong throughout their lives, they must hear, as Jesus' disciples did, of the reality of eternity. Jesus said that this world is passing away, that we will live with him in his kingdom for eternity, but also that eternity starts right now as we establish his spiritual kingdom in our hearts and learn to live with an eternal perspective.

How important it is that we give our children this perspective as we seek to lay the foundations for their lives. Jesus said, "Seek first His kingdom and His righteousness" (Matthew 6:33). We are to strain for heaven, to put our treasures there, and this means we must hold this world loosely.

If we teach our children through our actions or instruction, even subtly, that being successful in this world is somehow a measure of their importance and success, then we will miss the point of all the Lord's teaching. We are given one chance to live on earth, and the true measure of our success will be our faith, our faithfulness, and our obedience.

As I seek to teach my children all the biblical truths they will need to be equipped for life and also try to model for them a life of faith, eternal truth must always be the foundation of their understanding. If they can keep eternity before their eyes, they will be able to live in hope no matter what happens to them in this life.

And rest assured, something always happens! Happiness, after all, is elusive in this life. It is a sure thing that all the people our children love will die. All the material things they own will disintegrate. All the status they achieve will pass away.

But Christ and his kingdom will never pass away. He will be with us always. With this knowledge as the foundation of faith, our children will never lose hope and will never fail, because they have a future, "an inheritance which is imperishable and undefiled and will not fade away, reserved in heaven" for them (1 Peter 1:4).

May we see all of what we teach our children through this lens so that we might prepare them for our King and his eternal kingdom.

Chapter 10

Faith in a Living God

I couldn't put it off any longer. Settling into my desk chair with a strong cup of coffee, I determined that I would start my chapter on faith no matter what! There are so many aspects to faith, and it is such an important issue that I agonized over the project, wondering how I could convey faith in real-life, everyday terms that would motivate and inspire moms to pass on this important concept to their own children.

Just at that moment, the phone rang.

"Hi, Sally! It's Vickie. I have so much to tell you that I just had to call!"

Vickie and Tom are friends whose life story has had an encouraging impact on me. Watching them walk through their difficulties and challenges, which are far greater than those of almost anyone I know, has taught me a lot about what practical faith looks like. Vickie always has a gentle and quiet heart of praise for "all the wonderful ways God has shown us his faithfulness!"—even though at times it has been hard for me to understand what she means! To me, her circumstances have often seemed almost hopeless, yet she's kept a song on her lips for the Lord. Month by month, she and her family have lived out a testimony of faithfulness to God not only through their words but through their tenacious trust.

Tom and Vickie had enjoyed a good marriage and a pretty normal family life for a number of years. They found joy and fulfillment in raising their two children—a boy and a girl—and moving into their dream home had been the cherry to top it all off. Then, as their children grew older, Tom and Vickie developed a strong conviction that the Lord wanted them to have more children. The only problem was that Vickie had had surgery to prevent pregnancy. Reversing the procedure was possible, but it would cost twelve thousand dollars!

As Vickie and Tom spent time in prayer before the Lord, they sensed in their hearts an even stronger conviction that the Lord wanted them to have more children. They came to the conclusion that they should sell their lovely home, move into a smaller house, and use the extra money for the reversal surgery. Not long afterward Vickie became pregnant. The whole family was delighted with the prospects of having a baby in their home. However, Vickie soon miscarried this baby and then another. When she finally became pregnant for the third time, it was with much joy but guarded anticipation.

As soon as their precious little son Stephen was born, however, it was evident that he had severe health problems. A Down syndrome baby, he was born with heart problems and stomach problems and developed chronic lung problems very early.

Vickie and Tom were devastated. This is not at all what they had expected. But God spoke to them through his Word, urging them to have faith. They determined to hold fast to their precious Lord and believe that he "causes all things to work together for good to those who love God, to those who are called according to His purpose" (Romans 8:28).

Their constant prayer was one of trust: "Lord, we don't understand this, but we trust you to use Stephen's life for your glory!"

From the beginning, the doctors told them that little Stephen would surely not live. If, by some chance, he was able to stay alive, they said, he would never be able to walk and certainly would never be able to talk. Time after time, after each devastating prognosis, Vickie and Tom had to go on their knees before the Lord, choosing time and time again to believe he was with them and to trust him for their baby's future.

Over the next couple of years, little Stephen endured more than seventy hospital visits, heart surgeries, and stomach surgeries. His life was in constant danger. The monitors designed to alert them if he stopped breathing went off numerous times each night. Fatigue was a constant in their lives as my friends strove to care for their little son. At the same time, they struggled to meet the needs of their older two children, who not only had to adjust to less attention but be available around the clock to help with all that had to be done.

Tom and Vicki had decided they would take every opportunity to share with the doctors that they believed in a loving God who had a purpose for Stephen's life. Time and time again they were told by many doctors not to expect much and to remember that if he lived, he would never walk or talk. The evening of my phone call, Stephen had recently celebrated his fourth birthday.

"Sally, I have the best news for you! Stephen has been doing so well. As a matter of fact, he can now toddle and has taken eleven steps in a row. And guess what else? He can speak six words!" (In the past couple of months, as

I have been writing this book, Stephen has learned to walk around the block with great posture and agility and can speak twenty words!)

"But now, let me tell you the most amazing new result of Stephen's life! The doctors have been really impressed at how we've coped with all the problems. They actually are amazed that Stephen is still alive. So they've asked us to be available to come to the hospital whenever a Down syndrome child is born so that we can give counsel and comfort to the parents. Can you imagine? This has just opened wide a new door for us to share the Lord's love with people who really need it.

"Isn't God good?" she went on. "He has done so much through the life of our precious Stephen and brought such glory to himself!"

The glory has continued to unfold in the months since I received that phone call from Vickie. Not long afterward, for instance, I shared this story at a conference. A sweet young mom came up to me after the meeting with a three-week-old baby in her arms.

"You don't know how much that story encouraged me," she began. "This is our fourth child, and I didn't know how I was going to handle a new baby with the demands of all my other children. Well, now I know. If your friend can trust God in those circumstances, I know I can trust him in mine."

Even today, the blessings of Vickie and Tom's faith continue to spread out like ripples in a pond. For one thing, their second child decided to be a nurse after logging so many hours in a hospital with her little brother. And on top of it all, Stephen acquired a sweet, healthy little sister who toddles along with him now as they both improve their walking skills!

Who can know what impact the enduring faith in the lives of this one family will have? They have lived out the words of Hebrews 11:1-2: "Now faith is the assurance of things hoped for, the conviction of things not seen. For by it the men of old gained approval."

How have they done it? Step by step, certainly. I know they have not always felt victorious or strong. But they have been able to keep walking forward in faith because they know God well enough to trust his character. They know he is "compassionate and gracious, slow to anger and abounding in lovingkindness" (Psalm 103:8). They also understand that God is both loving and all-knowing, that he is in control and he knows what he's doing. And because they know this God, they've been able to look past their circumstances—the financial strain, life-threatening illness, exhaustion, discouragement. They've made a choice of their will to believe him for what they could not see at the time.

Even more important, Vickie and Tom have been able to keep walking in faith because they hungered to know God better, to walk with him daily. Hebrews 11:6 also tells us that without faith it is *impossible* to please God! It is the only prerequisite for a relationship with the Lord. By faith we are saved, by faith we please him, by faith we reap the gifts of his grace. As we walk in faith, therefore, our connection with God cannot help but grow stronger.

In my own life, there have been so many difficult seasons when I could not make sense of what was happening to me. Was it my fault? Had I displeased God in any way? Was it his fault? Did he even care? Did prayer really matter? How could these difficulties assail my life when I had been seeking to be so faithful to him?

How did I get through such seasons? Faith has had to carry me through each and every one. Faith is what gave me strength to take one more step when I had already gone as far as I thought I could go. I know that Vickie and Tom have often felt the same way.

My faith, though, wasn't just in thin air or in wishful thinking. The more I know about Christ and study his life, and the more I see the absolute integrity of his life, the more amazed I am at his character and love and his heart to reach out to us and help and redeem us. My faith is founded on the basis of God, his Word, his creation, and all that I know to be true about him.

As we look to the role of faith in the lives of the disciples, we see that Jesus constantly instructed them about it. He told them they could do the impossible, even move mountains, with only a tiny bit of faith (Matthew 17:20). He pointed out the power of faith in the lives of others—the Roman centurion (Matthew 8:5-13); a father named Jairus (Mark 5:22-24,38-42); a sick woman (Mark 5:25-34); blind Bartimaeus (Mark 10:46-52); a sinful woman (Luke 7:36-50); and many more. He also chastised the disciples occasionally for their lack of faith, such as when their boat was caught in a storm (Matthew 8:23-27). He told stories about faith and asked, "When the Son of Man comes, will He find faith on the earth?" (Luke 18:8). The issue of faith was constantly on his lips and in his instruction to help the disciples realize that knowing him and having a relationship with him and seeing answers to prayer were directly related to their faith in him.

The same is true for us, of course, which is why it is so essential for us parents to instill faith in our children. They are bound to experience many obstacles and difficulties in their lives. We cannot take away those circumstances, but we can offer our children the gift of faith so they will have the strength to live through them and a relationship with God that gives meaning to it all.

How do we go about giving our children the gift of faith? I will try to explain my perspective.

God has never taken all of my difficulties away. As a matter of fact, the more committed to him I have become, the more stress I seem to have. He has reminded me in Hebrews that "He disciplines us for our good, so that we may share His holiness" (12:10). He is concerned that I, his daughter, should have a strong, shining character, and such character requires training and discipline. As I walk through my circumstances and learn to shed some of my selfish attitudes and to work harder and to wait more patiently, the end result will be that I will be more like God. I will also see his faithfulness in my life as I see how he took me through the difficulties and brought me out of them. As I trust God to carry me through my problems, I actually learn to trust him more! And even more important, I become a living testimony of faith to others, especially to my children.

The best way we can give the critical gift of faith to our children, in other words, is to exercise faith in our own lives—to accept the difficulties of life and choose to trust God in the midst of them. This means we will choose to be thankful, choose to be joyful, choose to be mature and strong, and try to be an example for our children. It also means we will talk to our children about *why* we're choosing to respond in this way and share with them what God's Word says about faith.

This process gives them a pattern to follow in their own lives. When they are grown and far from our home and encounter a problem, they will remember, "When Mom and Dad had financial problems (or relationship problems or problems with us kids), they prayed about it, held on to God's promises, and waited with peaceful, faithful hearts for him to work. They trusted God, and it made a difference in their lives." Having grown up with such a model of faith will make it much easier for them to approach their own problems with faith.

But modeling is not the only way parents can teach faith to children.

Children also learn by observing the lives of others, as my children certainly learned by observing Vicki and Tom's family. Stories about men and women of faith—from missionaries and martyrs to quiet overcomers—can help move our children's hearts toward trust.

And of course the best stories of faith—as well as vital instructions—can be found in the New and Old Testaments. As we read the Bible with our children, we help them build an arsenal of faith to carry them through all future difficulties.

But we can't just hand them the Book (or read them a few verses) and expect them to understand it or do what it says. Having a Bible on their bedside table won't automatically help children develop a trusting relationship with God.

When Jesus called his disciples, after all, he didn't just hand them an instruction manual and leave them on their own. Instead, he lived beside them for three years—building a relationship, teaching them, repeating himself, correcting them, affirming them, showing them what to do and how to do it. Jesus taught the disciples to base their faith not only on the integrity of his words but also on the integrity of his faithfulness.

And this, I believe, is exactly what we must do with our children from the time they are small. We must teach them about faith, yes. We must live as examples of faith. We must urge them to do what's right, even if that means taking risky chances that make us a little nervous. (Teaching children trust means we must also trust him with their lives!) We must live close to them, building a relationship of trust, trying to be trustworthy ourselves. Most important, we must keep gently nudging them toward a relationship with the One whose very essence is loving faithfulness.

The gift of faith, remember, is not just wishful thinking but an accurate understanding of God's character and his integrity. Faith provides our children the security they need to step out in their lives, making confident decisions because they have developed a relationship with the God who is worthy of their trust.

Our children will face many trials even when they are young. So their childhood is the perfect time for us to take them by the hand and show them how they can walk through these difficulties with the Lord. Trusting him will become a natural, first response of children if they are raised from earliest childhood to pray to God and to walk with him each day of their lives.

How blessed is the child who is given the gift of faith by means of his or her parents' own faithfulness.

—A MOTHER'S PRAYER—

Faithful Father,

What a comfort it is to know you are in control and you can be trusted to work in all things for our good! Help us to live by faith, trusting you to work through the circumstances of our lives, so our children will learn to approach their own difficulties with faith in your faithfulness. Give us all the gift of faith so that we may walk through life with confidence, our hands in yours.

Amen

Chapter 11

Faith in God's Living Word

Tumbling out of the van on Sunday evening after two days of driving was a welcome relief to all of us, especially to the three who are six feet tall or over. (Riding together in a minivan these days has a different meaning for our family than when all my children were little.) But now that we were home, there was planning to be done. That evening found Clay and me poring over our calendars, trying to get a handle on all we needed to accomplish in the following four weeks.

We had just returned from a wonderful—and badly needed—family vacation in Florida. We had enjoyed a day together at an amusement park and spent some hours on the beach. Best of all, we had been invited to watch the launch of a space shuttle. The captain of the mission was Rick Husband, and his wife, Evelyn, is a friend of mine. So we had even been privileged to attend a prayer reception for Rick the night before.

What an inspiring time of worship and testimony that had been, with videotapes of Rick's life, magnificent music by Steve Green, and incredible pictures of outer space. Clay and I were asked to lead the corporate prayers for Rick, Evelyn, and their children, Matthew and Laura. And as we cried out in our hearts for God to give us the right words, Psalm 139 immediately came to mind.

"Lord," I prayed, "you have promised to be with us wherever we go, whether we ascend to heaven and take the wings of the dawn or dwell in the remotest part of the sea. Please help Evelyn and Matthew and Laura to remember while their husband and daddy is in outer space that you are with him. Help them to know that all of Rick's days are written in your Book. Thank you that you will be with him and protect him and be sovereign over his life because you have planned it."

As Clay began to pray, he, too, thought of a scripture: "Lord, help Matthew and Laura know that you desire to take them into your arms and bless them as you did the little children who came to you. Bless them, Lord, while their father is away, to feel the comfort of your arms" (see Matthew 19:14).

The morning of the launch had been perfect. As the space shuttle lifted off gracefully into an endless blue sky, a spontaneous round of applause had burst forth from all of us who were watching from the bleachers outside the space center. The moment had been filled with a sense of victory—a ship well launched. But now, just a few days later, we seemed to have thudded back to earth again.

I was already feeling stressed over suitcases to unpack, laundry to wash, e-mails to read, phone calls to answer, and a house waiting to be tamed the next morning. I had a feeling the next day—Monday—would be even worse. And it was.

"You know you have less than two weeks to prepare your new talks for the Michigan conference," Clay reminded me as he went out the door to his office. "And do you have time today to help me order books to sell at the book table? Also, I need someone to take my shirts to the cleaners…"

My husband's voice hadn't even faded before the litany of child voices began:

"Mom, we don't have any food in the house! What can we eat?"

"Mom, I can't find my NASA T-shirt, and I was going to wear it today! Can you help me find it?"

"Mom, I think the toilet's stopped up again. I can't get it to flush!"

"Mom, I need the car this morning! Can you stay here without a car for a while?"

The clenching of my stomach reminded me that we all needed to get our hearts in order before we tackled the tasks ahead. So I called the family together for a devotional time. And since Clay was already gone, I asked Joel if he would lead it. Though my older son was new at leading devotions, his sincere and strong heart lent strength to what he said:

"I have been reading a short passage this morning," he began when we had gathered in the living room. "It seems to apply to our lives just now. Philippians 4, verses 6 and 7. He held up his Bible and began to read: 'Be anxious for nothing, but in everything by prayer and supplication with thanksgiving let your requests be made known to God. And the peace of God, which surpasses all comprehension, will guard your hearts and your minds in Christ Jesus.'

"I think Paul knew we would be anxious about different areas in our lives," said Joel. (Boy, did he have that one right!) "But he tells us to take every single need that we have to God and leave it in his hands. Only then can we have the peace of Christ—when we have placed everything in his hands. He also tells us that this peace will guard our hearts and our minds. If you are letting God be God, then you will have a guard on your thoughts and feelings that will keep you from being anxious."

119

That was it—short and sweet. Joel led us in a prayer for our day.

"Lord, we give into your hands all the things that tempt us to be anxious. The busyness of the next few weeks. Mom and Sarah's conference in Michigan. The financial and administrative problems at the office. Our desire for friends. Lord, you know our needs. Thank you that in you we can have peace in each situation. Guard our hearts and minds through your Spirit as we trust in you. In Jesus' name, amen."

What a wonderful moment! My heart melted as my son ministered to me with heartfelt truth from God's Word that really helped me with my present needs. I had read that verse so many times before, but today it seemed to freshly apply. Off we all went to the duties of the day, sensing now that we weren't alone in the task.

But during the next ten days, before I was to leave on my trip to Michigan, a new crisis began to work its way through our home—the flu.

Nathan got it first. He had a high fever and slept on and off for three days. We took turns making soup and taking him tea and ginger ale and cool glasses of water. Next came Joel, who always takes things harder. He was practically lifeless, with a deep and rattling bronchial cough. I hated to even think about it, but I soon began to feel dizzy and lightheaded. Sunday afternoon found me with an irresistible need for a nap, and by Sunday night I had developed a fever.

For most of the next two days I stayed in bed, getting up only to give two ten-minute radio interviews, and those nearly wiped me out! By Wednesday I had totally lost my voice and was still feverish. Even directing the kids to pack my bags for the coming conference was a real effort.

"How am I going to speak this weekend, Lord?" I moaned that night. "I feel terrible!"

As I prayed for strength, God gave me my answer. Second Corinthians 12:9 came to my mind: "My grace is sufficient for you, for power is perfected in weakness." So did Philippians 4:13: "I can do all things through Him who strengthens me."

"Thank you, Lord, that you will be with me," I prayed as I drifted off to sleep. "Let your grace surround us every step tomorrow as we fly up to Michigan. Thank you for always promising to sustain me," I prayed as I went to sleep.

The next day irresistible sleep overtook me as I slumped in a groggy stupor on both legs of our flight. Sarah guided us both and all our luggage through two airports with ease and got us to our Grand Rapids hotel room, where I immediately crashed. By Friday evening, my voice was strong enough to deliver the passionate message the Lord had put on my heart, "Fulfilling the Mission of Motherhood."

In my speech I pointed to our experience just two weeks before with the shuttle launch in Florida and our friend Rick Husband, who had been very much on my mind as he went about his mission in space:

> Rick prepared for many years with his goal always in mind—
> to be able to go into outer space as an astronaut. Yet Rick
> knew that the most important event of his life was not becom-
> ing an astronaut, but giving the priority of his life to Jesus
> Christ. The real mission in his life was not just to go into
> outer space, but to glorify the Lord in everything he did. His
> testimony as a godly man, his relationship with his wife and
> children, and his desire to be a servant of God in all that he
> did was foremost in his mind. The Lord used Romans 12:1

to give him a pattern for his priorities: "Therefore I urge you, brethren, by the mercies of God, to present your bodies a living and holy sacrifice, acceptable to God, which is your spiritual service of worship."

We are responsible for launching our children into adulthood with the same purpose. Are we tempted to get distracted with the training and education and manners of our children as we parent them in our homes, even as Rick could have been distracted by the intense training he required to become an astronaut? Or do we understand that our mission is not just to train our children so that they can live good lives? As we launch them into adulthood, we are to reach their hearts for Christ and teach them how to be his representatives in the world so that in whatever they do, they will glorify him.

The next morning, as I was participating in a panel discussion, I heard my cell phone ring backstage. A few minutes later I glanced back there to see Sarah and several friends embracing each other with tears streaming down their faces. A few minutes later, as our speaking came to an end, I found out that the space shuttle *Columbia,* whose liftoff my family had watched in Florida, had exploded while reentering the earth's atmosphere. Rick Husband and the whole crew had lost their lives.

I was overcome with a palpable, heavy weight of deep sadness and loss. I thought of my sweet friend Evelyn and her precious children and immediately whispered a prayer for them.

Somehow we made it through the rest of the weekend and the flight home, but our astonishment and sense of disbelief at such an atrocious accident was a constant dark cloud hanging over our thoughts. It was still there when our family rendezvoused at the Nashville airport and I began to hear more about what had happened. Tears flooded our eyes as we all felt the grief of losing such a wonderful man of God and imagined the sadness that my friend and her children must be feeling.

I arose early the next morning to sneak some time alone in my little porch office. It was still dark outside, so I lit some candles, put on some soft music, poured myself a cup of tea, and sat in the stillness, trying to make sense of my confused thoughts. The chill of the cold morning air seemed to match the coldness I felt in my heart and the lump that seemed permanently wedged in my throat.

As the morning sun began to rise and my room gradually filled with soft light, I opened my Bible. "Sweet Lord," I prayed, "you have been my constant companion through so many different seasons of life. Give me some insight from your Word that will help me understand what has happened." I opened my Bible to Psalm 139:7-12, the same passage Clay and I had used to pray for the Husband family at the prayer reception:

> Where can I go from Your Spirit?
> Or where can I flee from Your presence?
> If I ascend to heaven, You are there;…
> If I take the wings of the dawn,…
> Even there Your hand will lead me,
> And Your right hand will lay hold of me.
> If I say, "Surely the darkness will overwhelm me,
> And the light around me will be night,"
> Even the darkness is not dark to You,
> And the night is as bright as the day.
> Darkness and light are alike to You.

Lord, I thought, *you were there with Rick when he took the wings of the dawn. You were there with him when he was flying in the starry heavens. Your right hand, your strong hand has hold of him. The darkness of this moment is not dark to you. You are with Evelyn and the kids even now.*

Next, I turned to John 11, which tells the story of Lazarus, the friend whom Jesus raised from the dead. All the way through the chapter, I was struck with how deeply Jesus mourned Lazarus' death. John 11:35 tells us that he wept. He was filled with sorrow when he saw Mary and Martha grieving.

Lord, you understand the sorrow of this terrible situation. You understand our sense of loss when difficult things happen.

Then I read Jesus' words in John 11:25-26: "I am the resurrection and the life; he who believes in Me will live even if he dies, and everyone who lives and believes in Me will never die." And my troubled heart began to ease as I realized the Lord had been with Rick all along and would also be with his family to comfort them as he had comforted Mary and Martha. Somehow, he was there. He would take care of my friends.

With a deep sigh I closed my Bible. I knew I would have other questions and feelings to take to him in coming days, but for now my heart was at peace.

And then, as I looked back over the past two weeks—our memorable vacation, the struggle afterward to catch up with our obligations, the flu, then the terrible news of Rick's death—I found myself pondering how important the Bible had been to getting through each moment. It had taken me through times of challenge, stress, illness, work, and grief. It had guided my thoughts and my words and equipped me for the tasks I was facing.

Through his Word, God had given me all I needed to live productively through the challenging circumstances he brought my way. He will do that for my children, too, which is why the Bible must be at the center of all we do as parents. One of the central ways we give our children the gift of faith is to base everything we do on the Word of God.

Psalm 19:7-8 reminds us, "The law of the LORD is perfect, restoring the soul; the testimony of the LORD is sure, making wise the simple. The precepts of the LORD are right, rejoicing the heart; the commandment of the LORD is pure, enlightening the eyes."

Jesus added to that idea by reminding his followers that his own words were a powerful foundation for life: "Everyone who hears these words of Mine and acts on them, may be compared to a wise man who built his house on the rock" (Matthew 7:24).

Jesus' disciples quickly learned that was true. His words became the guiding principles by which they lived and ministered the rest of their lives, and they took great pains to pass along to others what he had said. The four Gospels are really a collection of his most important words—recorded so that many could learn how to believe in him.

The Word of God gives our children the basis for their faith, a proper world-view, and wisdom and advice for all they will encounter. At the same time, it gives us the direction and instruction we need to be good mothers. In fact, it is as we apply God's Word to our everyday lives that our children will begin to understand its worth to us and to them.

How do we do that? In my experience, we give this gift of faith by making the living Word a natural part of our family life. Reading the Bible as a family, memorizing passages together and discussing how they apply to our lives, even letting kids act out Bible stories are ways to build faith by letting biblical truth permeate the fabric of our everyday existence. In addition, I believe, children must also see us studying our own Bibles and hear us mention ways the Bible helps us in situations we face. As they see that the Word of God makes a difference in our lives, they will be motivated to turn to the Word themselves. Eventually they may even become ministers of the Word to us, giving encouragement in the midst of our own need as my children did for me.

Making the Word of God the foundational source of instruction and training in our children's lives will ensure that, wherever they go the rest of their lives and whatever they encounter, God will lead them. His Word will go with them to instruct them. It is indeed a gift of faith we can give them that will help them the rest of their lives.

—A MOTHER'S PRAYER—

Giver of Life,
Thank you for giving me the opportunity to know you through the truth of your Word. Help me find time each day to read your Word and listen to what you would say to me through it. Show me ways to make your Word relevant in the small and big moments of my children's lives. Give them a hunger for your Word and an ability to understand it.

Amen

Chapter 12

Faith in the Spirit's Power

If everyone would just learn to put things up, we wouldn't have to spend an hour looking for keys!" one of my teenagers huffed while stomping loudly through the house. "This is a ridiculous waste of our time!"

We had been looking for the only set of keys still remaining in our home, the other sets having been previously lost. Having four drivers in the house now meant that no one could really blame anyone else for losing the keys, and no one would ever take responsibility!

"You were driving the car last! Where did you put them?"

"Well, you took them from my hand when you opened the back of the car to get groceries!"

"But you went to the store for milk after Dad got home!"

Ad infinitum!

So even though all of us had more important things to do, we stopped and looked in every possible nook and cranny for the keys, only to discover that they had fallen behind the refrigerator. No sooner had we gone to our various rooms after lunch, relieved that the key debacle was over, than we heard a crashing noise followed by a bang, bang, clatter that brought all of us quickly to the kitchen to see what bomb had exploded. There was our year-old golden retriever fairly smacking her lips as she wolfed down the last of three chicken breasts Sarah had cooked and left to cool on the stove while we first searched for the keys. Chicken broth and chicken pieces were all over the floor.

"Who let the dog in?" Again came the accusing voice of the same child who had made such a fuss before. (Teenage emotions were obviously running high that day.) "Doesn't anyone ever take responsibility around here?"

I sighed. Losing the keys was indeed irritating. Spilling a pot of chicken and broth and wasting expensive boneless chicken breasts to a greedy dog was exasperating. But the real problem we faced that morning was this particular child's haughty disposition and impatient accusations.

After the mess was cleaned up, I asked the offending child, the one with the *attitude,* to come to my room to talk. (Oh, those dreaded words: "Can you come to my room for a few minutes?")

We actually had a wonderful time talking. I was able to gain a better understanding of the pressure this teenager was feeling at this stage in life. And I ended up being able to compliment as well as caution:

"You know, I have been so encouraged by your life this year. You have filled in so many adult roles—going to the grocery store for me, chauffeuring kids to lessons and the gym, helping out with chores at home. But mostly I have been so encouraged by your growth in the Lord. It is so exciting to see your passion for him and the way you long for him to use you. I know he will do something special in and through you in his own time. But it is so easy to get excited about the big things and then allow yourself to blow it in all the mundane moments of life. If you give yourself license to get angry and frustrated every time you feel you can justify it, then you risk sacrificing your testimony as you grow older. Your spouse will grow to resent your outbursts, your children will be afraid of your anger, and your coworkers will learn to avoid you.

"I know, Mom," my now-chastened child mumbled. "And I'm really sorry for my attitude. I really will try harder. It's just so hard sometimes. I mean, it all seems so clear to me when I'm alone, but then something happens and…I just feel so explosive sometimes. And then I hate it when I let myself get out of control. You know what I mean?"

I nodded. I do know. But I also know—or at least I'm learning—the alternative to letting my emotions and my own sinfulness rule my life. "The Holy Spirit is in your life to give you his strength in these situations so that you can reflect his supernatural responses to life's demands. It's natural to let life irritate you and to get angry. It is *supernatural* to be patient and loving and gracious. That's really the secret to the Christian life—to learn to yield our lives and our emotions and our actions moment by moment to him. This is what Galatians 5:16 means: 'Walk by the Spirit, and you will not carry out the desire of the flesh.'"

"You know, Mom, I always start out in the morning deciding to be patient, but lately it has been hard!"

"I understand, honey. I do the same thing. I'm glad your heart is in the right place. Let's both pray for each other, okay?"

Our time ended with a satisfying teenage bear hug. I was so thankful to have been there for this important moment and grateful for the opportunity to teach my child one of the secrets from God's Word that so changed my own life and perspective. And what a privilege to witness one of those moments when the lights of God's truth seem to click on in my children's hearts, when the growth is almost visible. I know this will not be the last blast of inappropriate anger in the life of this child or any of my children—or in myself, for that matter. But I am confident we all are moving forward. Sometimes we stumble, but we are learning to trust the Spirit to move us forward. And this, too, is part of the gift of faith.

Later that week Sarah and I were on our afternoon walk near our home. We had been talking about the almost-overwhelming difficulties our family had experienced that year.

"I don't know how other people make it, Mom. I mean, people who aren't Christians. Every day, the Holy Spirit gives me just enough grace and light to make it through this day's struggles—just enough to give me hope and strength for this day as I need it. And I sure need it!"

She looked over at me, and I nodded. I found it interesting that the same subject would come up in our house twice in a week!

"It's all making so much sense to me these days," Sarah continued. "If a person tries to be good and live the Christian life on her own strength, she will run out of steam and crash. It can't be done on our own strength. I'm so thankful that I know the grace and forgiveness and freedom of trusting in the Holy Spirit to help me through each day."

I laughed aloud at this confirmation of what I had been thinking. Studying the ending chapters of John this past year had made a big impact on me recently. Though I had learned long ago the important principle of trusting God to live his life through mine by faith, I had really needed this refresher course on the work of the Spirit.

As I read through John 13–16, which contain the words Jesus spoke to the disciples the night before he was crucified, I had wanted to pay close attention to what he had said. I knew the last words people speak before they die are often important ones. How amazed I was to realize that just in these last hours of talking to his disciples, Jesus mentioned the Holy

Spirit at least nine times. He promised the Spirit would be sent after he himself had gone away. And he described this coming Spirit in a number of different ways—as the Helper (14:16), as the Spirit of truth (14:17), as a witness to Christ (15:26), as one who would guide them into all the truth (16:13), and as one who would be a reminder of his words (14:26). It was almost as if he used a lot of descriptions so he could be sure at least one would sink in.

I realized that if Jesus taught his disciples about the Holy Spirit with such intensity, he must surely have wanted them to understand that the Spirit would be very important to their lives in him. Thus, the Spirit is to have great importance in my life as well—in how I live and in how I teach my children.

In John 15:1-6 Jesus painted a vivid word picture of what it meant for the disciples to have their lives in him—to be filled with his strength and power through the Holy Spirit. He said, "I am the vine, you are the branches; he who abides in Me and I in him, he bears much fruit, for apart from Me you can do nothing" (verse 5). That's an eternal truth I must take to heart if I want to give our children the gift of faith.

To me as a parent, this "vine" reality has two implications. First, I must do what I can to stay connected to Jesus at all costs. Only when he lives through me will I have the patience, love, faith, strength, perspective, and understanding I need to raise godly, faithful children. Spiritual fruit in the lives of our children even depends—up to a point—on my staying connected to the Lord.

But the other side of this truth is that eventually my children must attach themselves to the Vine, not to me. Only the Lord can draw our children to himself. Only he can give salvation to our children. And only he can convict them of their sins. I can and must love my children, nurture them, comfort them, teach them. I can and must model for them what life as a "branch" looks like and show them ways to stay "attached" through prayer, Bible reading, fellowship with other believers, and so on. But I cannot be their "vine," and I cannot play the role of the Holy Spirit in their lives.

As my children have grown older, this realization has actually been a comfort to me. I cannot be with them everywhere they go. I cannot be right next to them the rest of their lives to tell them what to do. Even if it were physically possible to do so, such hovering would cripple them in their own abilities to become strong and wise. My children must learn how to walk with the Lord without my help. But they won't be alone. As Jesus promised, the Holy Spirit will be with each of my children every step of the way. He has access to their brains and their thoughts and their consciences, and he is committed to showing them the righteous way to go. Whenever I am worried—and I *do* worry, especially now that my teenagers are driving!—I can pray specifically for them, all the while knowing that even as I have a direct line to God, they have a direct line from him through the Holy Spirit. If I trust God to care for me, I must trust him to do the same for my children.

Knowing the limitations of my responsibility as a mother has actually been quite freeing to me. I can be God's agent for cultivating the hearts of my children; in fact, I'm supposed to fill that role. But only God can give them life, strength, and divine guidance. This means my success in life or in motherhood or as a Christian is not dependent on my being perfect, but on my allowing God, in the Person of the Holy Spirit, to work through me to accomplish his purposes. His life is far more powerful and authoritative than mine. As I depend on him, he who began a good work in me will perfect it (Philippians 1:6). He will do the same for the precious ones he has entrusted to me.

That understanding is one of the finest gifts of faith I can ever give my children. Even as I depend on the Lord, I must help them learn to depend on him. I must use as many ways as I can think of, as Christ did, to convey to them that none of us has to live the Christian life alone. We have Jesus' promise on that, and the Lord is always faithful to keep his promise. He will always be with us—mother and children alike—even to the end of the age!

—A MOTHER'S PRAYER—

Sustaining Spirit,
Thank you that you do not expect me to live the Christian life in my
own power. Help me to rest in your wisdom, trusting you to live your
life through me. Thank you that you will be with my children wher-
ever they go and that you have access to their hearts. Teach them to
respond to your comfort, guidance, and strength, and teach me to
trust you more with their lives.

Amen

For Study and Discussion

Giving Your Children the Gift of Faith

1. Read Psalm 119:105. According to this verse, what will give our children a proper foundation and guidance on their path of life? In what ways does this apply to our calling as ministers to our children?

2. Make a list of five things you could do to incorporate God's Word more effectively into your everyday family life. Pick one item from the list and commit to applying it faithfully for six weeks.

3. Hebrews 11:6 tells us that without faith, it is impossible to please God. What circumstances has God recently allowed in your own life that call for faith? In what ways are you modeling faith before the eyes of your children so that they are learning how to have faith in God?

4. Think of a time in the past when you have had to walk by faith but now look back to see what God has done. Tell your children about this experience in the form of a bedtime story. (If you can't think of a time in your own life, look for a children's book about faithful people. Or tell them the stories of Abraham and Sarah or Joseph in Egypt.)

5. According to Ephesians 2:8, what does God say is the source of our salvation? What does faith have to do with this? Do your children understand that God's love is a free gift with no strings attached? Plan out how you can communicate this principle to them.

PART FOUR

The Gift of Training

Godliness doesn't come naturally to any of us. We are born with a connection to God, a sense of his calling to us, but we are not born with knowledge of God's holy character and his ways. We are not born knowing how to live by biblical standards in the context of relationships, work, family, and the world. Growing in godliness and learning to apply wisdom in the context of daily life is a long-term process that requires instruction, practical application, and correction—sometimes a *lot* of correction! This process of training takes place in many different ways over a lifetime—from other people, from books, from the Lord's discipline. When children are small, however, parents are their primary sources of this necessary schooling in godliness. We are our children's first source for learning what it means to live for God in this fallen world.

Training leads us to share
in God's holy character.

Chapter 13

Persistent Miracles—a Model for Training

John and James sat heavily upon the ground beside Jesus with simultaneous deep sighs. Simon and Andrew joined them, while Thomas knelt to untie his sandal and rid himself of an irritating rock that had worked its way under his foot during the journey. An air of weariness hung about the little group. But it was a positive feeling, for they were weary from a job well done.

"You should have seen the people, Jesus!" Bartholomew exclaimed. "Everywhere we went, people followed us! We actually cast out some demons from a young boy who has been troubled all of his life!"

"And, Jesus, we anointed many sick people, just as you said, and many of them were healed!" Matthew's eyes were still glowing with the amazement of what he'd seen.

The apostles crowded around Jesus like excited children, eager to tell their amazing stories from their time of preaching and healing. But people there on the lakeshore were beginning to recognize them and crowd around, looking for miracles. The dull roar of voices soon drowned out even the apostles' own stories.

Jesus' authoritative voice captured their attention.

"Come away by yourselves to a secluded place and rest a while."

Recognizing their fatigue from being around throngs of people all day and ministering to their needs—they had even been too busy to eat!—Jesus motioned to the disciples to follow him. He pointed to a boat that had been pulled ashore and indicated that they should get in and row over to a less crowded part of the shore. But as the crowds of people saw the little group rowing across the lake, they ran ahead on foot and reached the secluded spot ahead of Jesus and the disciples. The disciples stared around with incredulity as they got out of the boat. There were thousands of men, women, and children crowded together on the hillside next to the water, watching Jesus and the disciples with eager, needy faces.

The disciples groaned, but Jesus' face softened, his compassion evident. Despite his own weariness, he began to teach them many things they longed in their hearts to know.

The disciples, who were by now at the strained end of weariness, finally pulled Jesus aside and pleaded with him. "This place is desolate and it is already quite late," Thomas said, pointing to the crowd. "Send them away so that they may go into the surrounding countryside and villages and buy themselves something to eat."

Then Jesus surprised them by saying, "You give them something to eat!" He gazed at them steadily, coolly, as if he had not just asked them to do something preposterous.

Judas rolled his eyes. Peter huffed and threw up his hands in frustration. John asked indignantly, "Shall we go out and spend two hundred denarii—a whole day's wage!—on bread and give them something to eat?" Didn't Jesus know how tired they were from doing God's work that day? Wasn't enough enough?

But Jesus ignored their body language. "How many loaves do you have?" Jesus asked. "Go look!"

They looked and reported impatiently back to him. "Five, and two fish."

Jesus then began to divide the people into groups and told them to recline on the grass. Soon the grassy hillside was covered with resting people, sitting in groups of fifty or one hundred, looking around expectantly. What was Jesus going to do?

Taking the small, woven basket in his hands, Jesus lifted up the round loaf of brown bread, raised his eyes toward heaven, and in a loud, steady voice offered up to his Father a blessing over the food he had been given. He then began breaking the loaf into smaller pieces. He piled the pieces into another basket, then reached for the next loaf. In just minutes, the basket was overflowing. It was taken out to the hungry crowd, and a new basket was put in its place. Then another basket was filled, and another. Calmly, quietly, almost mundanely, the miracle took place. Within an hour, five thousand men, along with their wives and children, had eaten from the plenty of Jesus' meal and were utterly satisfied, and the baskets were being filled with leftovers.

But Jesus hadn't forgotten the needs of his exhausted disciples. As soon as the leftovers were collected, he immediately motioned toward the boat and indicated that the disciples should head across the lake toward Bethsaida. The disciples hesitated—the wind was picking up, and the fishermen among them knew how quickly the weather could change. But one more look at the burgeoning crowd convinced them to follow their Master's suggestion. They rowed away from shore as Jesus, who remained behind, began bidding farewell to the people who had stayed to hear him speak.

Jesus sent the crowd away with full stomachs and overflowing hearts. Then, with a heavy sigh, he turned his face toward a nearby mountain where he loved to pray. Weary, empty, and needing to be alone, Jesus climbed the slope under the stars and settled down for a long session with his Father.

Much later in the evening, while Jesus sat in the peace of prayer on the hillside, he looked out and saw the disciples' boat still out on the water. It had hardly moved, even after many hours. Jesus arose and began to walk down the mountain to be with his beloved friends. He reached the shoreline. And then he kept walking…

By the middle of the night, the disciples were weary beyond measure. All night long they had struggled at their oars against a powerful headwind, and at this point they were debating whether they should just turn around and go back. They certainly weren't expecting to see the dark silhouette of a stranger walking on the water, and they cried out in terror when they saw him approaching.

"Take courage; it is I, do not be afraid," came the confident, calm voice of their Master over the gale. They stared with disbelieving eyes wide as Jesus walked across the swirling waters and climbed into the boat with them. And then, immediately, the wind stopped!

The disciples were astonished, for they had not gained any insight from the incident of the loaves. They just sat there in the now-still boat, incomprehension clouding their features, too stunned even to ask questions.

Jesus gave them a little smile and shook his head as he settled into the boat to complete the journey. They still had no clear understanding of who he really was and why he was there. But soon enough, he knew, they would understand.

Just a week or two later Jesus was again speaking to a large group of people when he called on the disciples to bring him any food they could find. Once again, from seven loaves of bread and a few fish, Jesus fed a huge group of men, women, and children—four thousand this time. And once again, the disciples climbed into a boat to go to the other side of the lake. This time Jesus went with them. But a murmur of grumbles soon arose as they realized they had fed so many others and had forgotten to bring enough leftovers to feed themselves.

Hearing their complaint, Jesus turned to them with something slightly harder than usual in the depths of his eyes. Like a mother who is weary with her children's immaturity, Jesus addressed his disciples: "Why do you discuss the fact that you have no bread? Do you not yet see or understand? Do you have a hardened heart?... When I broke the five loaves for the five thousand, how many baskets full of broken pieces did you pick up?"

"Twelve," they said.

"When I broke the bread for four thousand, how many large baskets full of broken pieces did you pick up?"

"Seven," they said.

He waited, looking at them, waiting for the light to dawn. It didn't. They just stared back at him, perplexed.

"Do you not yet understand?" he repeated. And then he sighed. He had worked so hard to train them, not only with his words, but with his actions.

When would they ever learn?[1]

The disciples were the best men Jesus could find to follow him—strong, committed, and sincere in every way. They had dropped their fishing nets and left their businesses to follow him. These were the people he had designated to be responsible for his worldwide ministry when he died. He spent three years of his life training them. Why, he even enlisted them in his work of teaching, casting out demons, and healing the sick. With their own eyes, they saw him feed the multitudes and even walk on water. And yet again and again, they failed to comprehend what they saw. Jesus even told them directly who he was and what would happen, yet they still couldn't get their minds and hearts around it.

"Their heart was hardened" is the way the Bible puts it in Mark 6:52. Still new in their faith, the disciples were unable to comprehend what it meant that Jesus was the Son of God, even though they had lived with him, known him intimately, and participated in his miracles. Even the night before he died, Jesus was still trying to get through to them (John 14:1-9).

"Lord, we do not know where You are going," said Thomas as they ate their Passover meal together. "How do we know the way?"

Jesus must have sighed. But he spelled it out patiently: "I am the way, and the truth, and the life; no one comes to the Father but through Me."

But then Philip asked, "Lord, show us the Father, and it is enough for us."

"Have I been so long with you, and yet you have not come to know Me, Philip?" His frustration was evident by this time. "He who has seen Me has seen the Father."

But the good news about Jesus' disciples was that after he died and rose, all those hours of careful training finally kicked in. At last they grasped the reality of who he was and what he had come to do. And in the years after Jesus' ascension, they became exactly the kind of people Jesus wanted to advance his kingdom. They remembered his words and shared them with others and even wrote them down. They drew on his gift of the Holy Spirit to preach the gospel and heal the sick and minister to the poor. As Jesus had predicted, they became his witnesses throughout the earth— every single one of them except Judas—and they did it so effectively that together they turned the whole world upside down. Ancient church tradition tells us that each of the disciples died a martyr's death except John, and he suffered greatly for his testimony.

So how does all this apply to motherhood? To me, it's a comforting reminder that any kind of training takes time, patience, and endurance. If Jesus himself had trouble getting through to his disciples—even with miracles!—we human parents shouldn't be surprised when the process of training our children hits some difficulties.

Our children must be taught so much in their time with us. We want them to learn gracious manners so they can behave in a civilized manner and also witness effectively to those who come into their lives. We want them to be responsible with their work (chores, homework, jobs, money, time, possessions) and with their lives (their grooming, behavior, relationships with others, moral decisions). We certainly want them to grow spiritually, to learn habits of Scripture study, prayer, and fellowship, and to develop godly character traits such as honesty, compassion, trust, and obedience.

But the process of instilling these traits in our children through training can sometimes feel like an exercise in futility. We explain and advise (and repeat ourselves a lot). We encourage and cheer. We correct mistakes and misbehavior. We *make* mistakes as well, because we are fallible, inconsistent human beings ourselves. And then we start the whole process over the next day:

"No, you may not talk to your sister that way! Try it again!"

"How many times do I have to tell you to pick up your socks?"

"I would appreciate it if you would always bring your dishes to the sink after a meal and put them into the dishwasher."

"What does 1 Corinthians 13 say about love?"

"Okay, I want you to do it again, and this time use soap."

Even as Jesus had to be patient with fully grown but spiritually immature men who seemed slow to respond to his training, so we must practice patience with our children—and ourselves. The very nature of training is that it usually involves immature individuals, which means it takes a long time to accomplish its goals!

Yet Jesus' experience with his disciples can also encourage us to persist, because we see that the long, frustrating process of training really does make a difference. No matter how futile the process may seem at times, most children eventually learn the truths and habits we are diligent to instill in them. As Proverbs reminds us, if we "train up a child in the way he should go, even when he is old he will not depart from it" (22:6).

It is so fulfilling for me to finally be at the age where I can see this happening. Our older children are just now turning the corner toward adulthood. As they become more responsible and take on more of our values and convictions, I have to laugh as I see them respond to my younger children:

"Mom, Joy makes such a mess when her friends are over here to play. She needs to learn to clean up!"

I think to myself, *You were twice as messy, and I never thought you heard a thing I said!*

In the tenth chapter of Hebrews, the writer admonishes his readers to keep on believing. These Christians were deeply discouraged from seeing firsthand the persecution and death of fellow believers. They must have felt there was no hope left for them. But the Hebrews writer urged them on with a message that also applies to parents seeking to train their children: "Therefore, do not throw away your confidence, which has a great reward. For you have need of endurance, so that when you have done the will of God, you may receive what was promised" (verses 35-36).

God designed us not only to be the "civilizers" of our children, but also to raise disciples for him and prepare them for kingdom work. We are to be their consistent, loving, persevering trainers, and this means we must persevere in hope, even when we don't seem to be going anywhere. Even as Jesus was greatly glorified by the eventual faith of his disciples, we can expect our diligence to be greatly rewarded by the development of strong character in our children. This gift of training will serve them their whole lives as they walk faithfully and boldly in the footsteps of the One who fed the multitudes, calmed the seas…and managed to turn a group of bungling, immature men into true apostles.

Chapter 14

Training Children
to Think

The world has always been a scary place. And in this day of large-scale disasters like September 11, "orange-level" terrorist threats, front-page kidnappings and sniper attacks, even exploding spacecraft (by the time you read this, you will have new events to add to the list!), there's a lot to trouble the minds of young children.

Clay and I have always had a deep desire in our hearts to keep our little ones innocent and pure as long as we can, helping them develop a sense of security by protecting them as much as possible from the knowledge of such events. I do not want to burden them with crises and issues that are too much for them to understand or bear. A pure, unscarred conscience and joyful set of childhood memories is a gift I want to give to all our children.

But the truth is that no matter how vigilant I am, I cannot protect them from everything. And I've found that sheltering our youngest child from troubling information is even more difficult than protecting the others was. With three siblings who are interested in world events and eager to discuss them at dinner, for instance, it's hard for seven-year-old Joy *not* to be aware of disturbing headlines. And then there's the assorted information she gets from friends—a neighbor down the street convinced her there were men in the area who could come into her bedroom and kidnap her, and another child told her a sniper was in our neighborhood, shooting anyone he could find. The loss of our family friend Rick Husband in a space-shuttle explosion was a blow we couldn't shield her from. And after the war with Iraq began in 2003, Joy heard some adults talking about the terrible things Saddam Hussein had done to his own countrymen who disagreed with him.

The final blow came one evening at a friend's house, where a group of parents were discussing a child-abuse case that a lawyer who was present had defended. I hadn't even known Joy was in the room until she crawled up into my lap and whispered, "When I get to be an adult, I'm only going to talk about fun things and not all those boring, bad things."

About this time Joy began to have bad dreams on a nightly basis. Welcoming her into our bed with us was becoming a habit. One evening as I was helping her put on her nightgown and get ready for bed, she got a very serious look on her face. "Mommy, sometimes I dread going to sleep because I'm afraid I will have a bad dream that will scare me again!" We talked about her dreams and prayed for the Lord to "keep her from the evil one." Each night after that, I lay down with her before she went to sleep.

As I thought about the problem, though, I realized that fear was a pattern Joy had displayed since she was very young. It wasn't just that she had been exposed to a lot of difficult things that were happening in the world.

She was also a sensitive, highly imaginative child who took life seriously. She felt very guilty if she did anything the least bit wrong. She was extremely fearful of anything happening to our family. And she could hardly stand conflict of any kind.

As I prayed about all these issues, the Lord brought to my mind the way he had helped his disciples with difficult issues in their lives. Once they chose to follow him, after all, the disciples faced frequent ridicule and derision. They were sometimes in physical danger. They had to cope with family problems (such as a sick mother-in-law) while being on the road full time with the Lord. And of course they faced the mundane issues of arranging for food and shelter as they traveled. Sometimes they were cold or hot or hungry, and they were often weary and worried.

What did Jesus do when the difficulties arose? He certainly didn't take his disciples out of the world or try to shelter them from difficulties. In fact, Jesus even raised *new* issues for the disciples to think about. He talked to them about the end of the world. He told them there would be "wars and rumors of wars" (Matthew 24:6). He predicted famines and earthquakes and wars between nations. He also told his followers that "they will deliver you to tribulation, and will kill you, and you will be hated by all nations because of My name. At that time many will fall away and will betray one another and hate one another.... But the one who endures to the end, he will be saved" (verses 9-10,13).

Jesus never tried to pretend that scary things were not going to happen. (They did!) Instead, he prepared his disciples for difficulties by training them how to *think* about what happened to them. He reminded them that even as the Father cared for birds and flowers, they could trust God to care for them. He promised he would always be with them. He prayed specifically that the Father would not take them out of the world but would keep them from the evil one. And he gave them hope by reminding them that though they would have trouble in the world, he had overcome the world. If they remained faithful to him, they would emerge from tribulation into triumph.

Jesus prepared his disciples to respond wisely to tribulation by instructing them and training them how to think about what happens from his perspective, and I could do this with Joy as well. As Paul indicated to the Corinthians, she needed to be "destroying speculations and every lofty thing raised up against the knowledge of God, and…taking every thought captive to the obedience of Christ" (2 Corinthians 10:5). By helping her develop a habit of thinking biblically about her own little-girl fears, I could reduce her stress in the present. In the process, I could also prepare her to think clearly and wisely as an adult, when she would encounter much more daunting challenges.

"Joy," I said to her one night, "Jesus tells us that Satan is the prince of this world. Because this world is in rebellion to God and his ways, sometimes terrible things happen. I can't always take those terrible things out of your life. But he did tell his disciples that he would be with them. He also told them not to be afraid. He even told them not to be afraid of Satan. But in order to not be afraid, we have to train ourselves to reject all the thoughts that cause us to be fearful. We have to train our minds to think the right thoughts, to believe the things that Jesus told us are true. And I can help you learn to do that, but I can't do it for you.

"What you have to do is try to capture every bad thought you have and sort of put it in jail. Then you need to fill your thoughts with the true things he has promised. This is a way you can become strong in your faith in Jesus. Jesus even told his disciples that the Holy Spirit would guide them into all the truth. Jesus knows that what you think will determine how you feel and how you act."

Joy pondered this for a moment, and I continued.

"You know, sweetie, you can't keep a bird from flying over your head. But you would never let a bird build a nest there, would you?"

Joy giggled at that idea.

"Well, in the same way," I said, "you can't keep some bad thoughts from coming to your mind, but you can keep them from staying there. And maybe the two of us can think of some creative ways to help you keep the good thoughts in and the bad thoughts out."

Together we asked the Lord to give us some ideas, and then we got to work. First we found a string of tiny white lights and strung them on her headboard to provide a little more light in the room. Then we pulled out one of the little gold angels we had given as gifts at a Christmas mother-daughter tea. Joy decided it might help to hang hers near the lights on her headboard.

Snuggling together on her bed that night with blankets tucked in around our necks, we admired Joy's lights and her angel. Together, we decided it was a guardian angel from the Lord to watch over her while she was sleeping and to protect her thoughts. She seemed satisfied in her heart with her new "protectors" and fell quickly and peacefully to sleep.

The next morning as I was stirring oatmeal at the kitchen stove, Joy ran in and threw her little arms around my waist, hugging me with all the strength she could muster.

"Mommy, I've been thinking!"—a common statement from Joy! "I think that really God sent *you* as my guardian angel, to stand over me, to protect me, to tell me all the truth you know about God, and to guide me everywhere I go. So I have my angel on the bed, but I have you to be my 'always with me' angel!" Plying me with a couple of enthusiastic wet kisses, she turned and skipped away with a smile on her face.

It struck me later, as I pondered the truth of her proclamation, that God has indeed called me as a mother to be an "angel" watching over my little children. Then I found myself wistful, wishing I had my own "angel mother" nearby to watch over me. But the Lord reminded me that I do have such a guardian and guide in the Holy Spirit. The Lord knew that as an adult I would have recurring fears, questions about life, pressures and needs that would require the help of someone more mature, capable, and more prepared for life than I—someone who can help me guard and focus my own thoughts.

As a mother, in other words, I, too, have a need to "walk in the Light as He Himself is in the Light," as John reminded Jesus' followers (1 John 1:7). I need to give my thought processes to the Lord—to reject fear and focus on the reality of the Lord's love and power. As I model such disciplined thinking for my children and as I train them how to think for themselves, I not only arm them for their future spiritual battles; I also arm myself.

Jesus spent most of his time as recorded in the Gospels teaching his disciples how to think. As we give our children the gift of a trained mind, we will give them the ability to resist temptation when we are not with them, to overcome fear when Satan whispers lies in their minds, to rely on the Holy Spirit when they need wisdom. The mind is a muscle that must be exercised and correctly trained, but a well-trained mind makes it so much easier for the heart to follow Christ in faith. When it comes to protecting and preparing our children for all that will happen in their lives, the gift of a disciplined mind is one that truly keeps on giving.

–A MOTHER'S PRAYER–

Eternal Word,

Help us as mothers learn to think biblically, to apply your truth and your perspective to all areas of our lives. Give our children a love for your Word so they may always look to the Bible to give them light for their paths. Help us train our children to discipline their thoughts so they may learn to love you with all their minds. As they internalize your truth, let them show forth your light to others who need so desperately to hear and understand your ways.

Amen

Chapter 15

Training Children to Pray Effectively

Spring fever threatened to be the undoing of this book. My small sun-room/office has windows on three sides that give a sweeping view of our three-acre backyard. And thanks to the labor of the woman who lived here before me, our yard looks to me like the garden of some old English manor. Though I don't know the woman personally, I am so thankful for her. She lived in this home for seventeen years before we moved here, and in that time she planted hundreds upon hundreds of bulbs—a wide variety of jonquils and daffodils, irises, and lilies, as well as pink and red antique roses, redbud trees, forsythia bushes, peach and pear trees, dogwoods, and many other flowering treasures.

Right now is the height of the daffodil season. What seems like at least a thousand flowers fill the yard, which is also dotted with sweeping forsythia. Yellow and green are definitely the color of the hour! The velvet green of lush, new grass is covering the small hills I can see right out my window, calling me to abandon my dull, gray computer and come outdoors.

It strikes me that through her years of hard work and faithful tending, the woman who lived here before me has left a legacy of beauty that will bless many people for years to come. I made no effort to cultivate these flowers. It was her investment of digging the earth, planting the flowers, tending and fertilizing them, that is now bearing fruit and brightening my life.

As I was thinking about what to write while gazing out my windows, Joy and Nathan popped in my room.

"Mom, guess what. The war with Iraq has started!"

Well, so much for my peaceful reverie! We were talking about this huge event and what it might mean when Clay came into my room. He was home much earlier than normal from his day at the office.

"I just found out that the brochures for the conferences have not reached our mailing list in Tennessee," he pronounced with a look of concern in his eyes. "We might have to cancel the conference! Also, the five thousand brochures that were supposed to go out to Texas have been sitting on the dock at the post office for over a week because of a mix-up at the mailing office. And no one ever called and contacted us! This could mean a real financial crisis. I've already ordered lots of materials for the conferences, and the brochures alone have cost a pretty penny! I came home to see what you think we should do."

My response was immediate and heartfelt: "Get all the kids together and let's have some time of prayer for the country and for our ministry!"

It was such a sweet, familiar scene as we all gathered in the living room. Sarah and Joel sat on the leather couch while Joy and Nathan plopped down on the floor with Kelsey, our beloved and "soft to pet" golden retriever. Clay and I took the other couch.

"We praise you, Lord, that you have chosen us to be your children and that you are a loving Father," Clay began. "Thank you that we can always come to you with every detail of our lives, knowing that you hear us and want to respond to our needs and desires."

After that beginning, we took turns praying about all that was on our hearts.

The older children's prayers were pointed and bold; a sense of fresh idealism filled their voices. Nathan's quick, straight-to-the-point prayers seemed to say, "I know you are listening, Lord, and here's what is on our hearts!" Little Joy's prayers came from a fervent, innocent heart that believed in her Lord's ability to "part the Red Sea" for us in whatever way he wanted. "But only do what you want to in our lives, Lord, 'cause we love you a lot!" This time, I was on the end, and I tried to wrap up our time together with the sense of thankfulness that had filled my heart as I looked out on our beautiful gold-and-green landscape.

After we closed our prayers, Joy followed me back to my office. "You know," she said, "I was just thinking about how every mother of every soldier in the war is going to pray that her child doesn't get hurt. But you know some of them are going to get killed anyway. So how do you know how to pray the right way? You can't always get the answer you wanted, so why pray?"

"Joy, I was just reading about prayer in my Bible time today. Can I tell you a couple of things I have learned?"

She sat next to me as I pulled out my Bible to show her the words.

"It says in Luke 11 that Jesus' disciples came to him and asked him to teach them how to pray, because they didn't have all the answers either.

That's when he taught them the Lord's Prayer that we learned earlier this year. It's in the book of Matthew, too. Jesus taught it to people as part of the Sermon on the Mount. Let's look at it there."

Joy snuggled closer as I turned to Matthew 6, and we examined the Lord's words together:

> Our Father who is in heaven,
> Hallowed be Your name.
> Your kingdom come.
> Your will be done,
> On earth as it is in heaven. (verses 9-10)

"Let's just take this part today," I told Joy. "Now, see, the first thing Jesus said to do is acknowledge God's position in heaven. That means we recognize he is King of the universe and he rules over all the details of our lives. Next, Jesus tells us to remember that God's nature is holy and perfect—that's what *hallowed* means. He can't make any mistakes."

Joy nodded briskly. "I know that already."

"You know a lot already," I said. "Anyway, then Jesus tells us to pray 'Your kingdom come. Your will be done,' and that means we should pray with a heart of understanding. Sometimes we act like the point of prayer is to try to persuade God to give us what we want. It's like we are begging God to do our will, to do what we want him to do.

"You know how Mommy hates it when one of you kids begs me for something you know I have already said no to?"

Joy nodded emphatically.

"Well, the reason I have to sometimes say no to your request is that I know what you have asked for isn't going to be good for you, or sometimes it doesn't fit into the plans Daddy and I have for the rest of the family. Well, sometimes God has to say no too. But he still wants us to always come to him because he loves us to trust him and look to him to be our loving Father who provides for us. And that's what prayer is really for. It's so we can talk to God as a personal and treasured friend, just like you would come to Daddy or me because you know we love you. We are supposed to come to him with a heart that says, 'God, I want your will to be done in my life and in this situation. Help me to be willing to be a part of what you have already planned. I know that what you have planned is right and good because you are holy and perfect.' You see what I mean?"

Joy pondered, thinking hard. "So we're supposed to pray because God loves us, even if we don't get what we pray for?"

Her directness made me smile. "We know God will take care of us and do what is right and according to his plans. But we're supposed to pray because God loves us and wants us to stay close to him, and the best way to stay close is to talk to him all the time. Jesus told his disciples many times during his life that he wanted them to pray to God about everything. Sometimes God does use our prayers to change the world. But no matter what, it always pleases him greatly when we pray."

Immediately, the Lord brought to my mind the flowers outside the windows of the room where we were talking.

"You know, sweetie, as you look out to the beautiful flowers in the yard, we get lots of pleasure from their beauty just because they are all around us. But they didn't just accidentally happen. Someone had to take the time to plan the garden and buy the seeds and the bulbs and the bushes and trees. Then someone had to take the time to dig up the yard, plant the seeds, water them, and wait for them to grow. Now, we're enjoying the fruit of that hard work.

"Prayer can work like that too. We have to take time to pray, to go to God day after day. We praise him for his beauty and wonderful character. We acknowledge that he is King of the universe and in control of everything. We ask him to take care of our needs, and we tell him our desires. We take the time to plant seeds of faith with God in heaven. And we don't always see the fruit of our faith right away. But we know if we wait, we will see the answers to our prayers, just as we see these flowers, and other people will see them too. We will see the great works of God in our lives and be thankful for the times when he gave us the desire of our heart. But the results of our prayers will be a whole lot more than just wishes granted. We'll have a picture of beauty in our hearts and in our relationships and in our work for the rest of our lives, because we took the time to do the faithful work for God's kingdom that he asked us to do. When we take the time to pray as Jesus told us to, our faithfulness in prayer will cause wonderful things to happen in our lives and even all over the world. Sometimes we just have to wait awhile to see it."

Joy loves real stories, and she loves to pick our many flowers. She kissed my cheek and said, "That makes sense, Mommy. I can't wait to see what God does!"

As she ran through the door to go outside, I remembered that Jesus had also used flowers to instruct the people who came to hear him teach. "Consider the lilies…," he had said not long after he taught the disciples his prayer. So I felt like I was in good company and could now imagine that Jesus had been teaching this on a green-and-gold day much like mine.

As I searched my Bible concordance that morning under the words *pray* and *prayer,* I was reminded once more of prayer's importance to Jesus. His words to the disciples were often about prayer—not just his model "Lord's Prayer," but also the idea of praying "for those who persecute you"

162

(Matthew 5:44), praying in secret to be seen only by God (Matthew 6:6), praying in faith (Matthew 21:22), and praying with humility and repentance (Luke 18:10-14).

Even more important, though, is that his disciples saw Jesus pray many times in many situations. Prayer was a constant for him, the heartbeat of his life. He often went up to the mountains or out at night so he could be alone and pray: before choosing his disciples (Luke 6:12-13), after feeding the five thousand (Mark 6:41-46), and many other times. He prayed when Lazarus was raised from the dead (John 11:41-44), at the Transfiguration (Luke 9:28-29), in the garden of his betrayal (Matthew 26:42), and even from the cross (Luke 23:33-34).

Jesus lived to be in communication with God. And so must we if we are to give our children the gift of training in prayer.

As our children observe our lives, they are quick to notice if we are hypocritical. They know if we talk a lot about prayer but rarely pray. Since Jesus spent so much time teaching his disciples to pray, we must take time with our children to teach them about prayer and to answer their questions. But even more, prayer must be a regular habit of our everyday lives. As we model prayer, we train our children regularly to come to God in faith. As they hear our teaching and watch us doing what we taught them, our children will pick up this habit with ease.

I have often been in situations where people have said, "Oh, I could never pray in front of people." Yet Jesus did it constantly before the disciples, in a natural way. He even told them not to worry too much about the actual words—just to pray from the heart.

If we desire to help our children grow in spirit and enjoy an intimate walk with God, then prayer must have the same priority in our lives as it did in the life of Jesus. Training our children in prayer will open the windows of heaven into their souls as they gradually learn to come to their heavenly Father each day.

–A MOTHER'S PRAYER–

Dear Heavenly Father,
We are so grateful that you are always ready for us to come before
your throne to find mercy and grace in time of need. Let us model a
life of praise and prayer so that our children learn to come to you
each day with all the issues of their lives. Teach us also to hear your
voice as we worship you in our prayers, that we may know how to do
your will. We want to know, just as the disciples wanted to know,
how to pray to you and trust you with our lives.

Amen

Chapter 16

Training Children
for Tribulation

Joel has been singing melodies and making up songs since he was a toddling little boy. I remember him singing the "ABC Song" perfectly in tune when he was eighteen months old. He continued to sing and hum songs into his elementary-school years and landed his first solo part in a children's play when he was five years old.

It was no surprise to us, then, when eleven-year-old Joel tried out for a prestigious boys' choir and got in.

The director of music came out singing his praises. "This boy has more raw talent than anyone I have ever tested!" he exclaimed emphatically. "It's important that you be good stewards of his ability and place him in a musical setting!"

We were thrilled at the possibilities the Lord seemed to be opening up for Joel, and we jumped right into the whirlwind of activity this new opportunity presented. We began the routine of taking Joel for long after-noon practices so he could join the beginners' group of the traveling choir. We allowed him to be involved in a Christmas production that required many nights of rehearsals. We all attended his performances as a family. (The group of boys in their grown-up navy blazers, red ties, and gray flannel pants did look quite striking and truly sounded like angels!) And at first, Joel reveled in the whole process of learning and performing. Gradually, though, we saw his joy begin to fade.

One evening as we dressed him up for one of the evening perfor-mances, I noticed he was very quiet and pensive.

"Are you feeling okay, Joel?" I asked.

"I'm okay, Mom," was his quiet response.

I told myself he was just tired of the constant rehearsals and all he needed was a good night's sleep to be his normal self again. But my con-cern persisted, and the next day, as we munched our breakfast toast, I ques-tioned Joel again.

"How was your performance last night? Are you still enjoying being in the group?"

His face fell, and he finally told us what had been bothering him. "There's this older guy in the group, and every day when I go to practice, he gets me off in the corner and bullies me. He tells me I'm a loser and the sorriest excuse for a person he's ever met. Then he says no one can under-stand how I made it into the choir. I used to think I could just ignore him, but it's starting to bother me, and I don't even enjoy going anymore."

As we probed into the situation, we found out the young man had called Joel names I can't repeat. The young man evidently was struggling with anger over his father's having left home and his parents' divorce, and he was taking out his rage on Joel and some of the other new boys.

Joel tried hard to be gracious to the needy boy and sought to have a peaceful relationship. No matter what he did, however, things didn't seem to get better.

In the meantime, I was really struggling with the situation. As a mother, I resented the fact that this boy was making it so hard for my son to do something he had always wanted to do. With all my heart, I wanted to protect Joel from mean people; I wanted to save him! I struggled to find an easy solution and couldn't think of any.

Late one evening after I had put the other children to bed, Joel knocked lightly on our door and asked to talk to Clay and me. "You know," he said, "we have talked so much over the years about learning to love people and reach out to them. I always thought that would be easy to do. But trying to be nice to this guy who just keeps giving me a hard time has really been hard. It just doesn't seem fair. I haven't done anything wrong, and *I'm* the one who keeps having to try to make things right."

Clay met my eyes. To be honest, we had been thinking the same thing!

But Joel went on: "Anyway, I was just lying in bed thinking that maybe this guy feels real bad about his dad leaving him—I mean, *I* would feel really awful—and maybe he doesn't have anyone to make him feel accepted. And I was thinking about what it must have been like for Jesus to die for people even when they rejected him and didn't know he was dying for them. It cost him a lot. So I guess if I want to be his follower, it will cost me a lot too. I want to be strong, so I think I need to pray for Mike and try to keep being nice. Maybe he'll see a difference in me and some-day I can help him!"

It was quite a long speech for a young boy to make, and by the time it ended, Clay and I were smiling. We realized that the Lord had allowed this situation to teach our son an eternal truth and to remind us once more of the truth we already knew—that the cost of discipleship, the cost of being a follower of Christ and holding on to his ideals, can be high indeed. Joel was learning that even as a boy he could make godly choices in the midst of unfair accusations. He was also learning a great lesson about what it means to choose to be involved in others' lives for the sake of Christ. The truth of Matthew 10:38-39 was coming alive for him: "And he who does not take his cross and follow after Me is not worthy of Me. He who has found his life will lose it, and he who has lost his life for My sake will find it."

Jesus was always very clear with his disciples that following him would cost them something—sometimes a lot. In John 16:33, he told the disciples plainly that "in the world you have tribulation." Earlier in the book, in John 15, Jesus said, "If the world hates you, you know that it has hated Me before it hated you" (verse 18) and "Remember the word that I said to you, 'A slave is not greater than his master.' If they persecuted Me, they will also persecute you" (verse 20).

If we raise our children to be Christians, Jesus' words apply plainly to them as well. And as a mother with a nurturing heart, I find this hard to take. I have such a desire to protect my children and smooth the road for them, and I know you feel the same about your children. And I believe we're supposed to feel this way. Protecting children is part of our God-ordained task of mothering and also, according to Matthew 18:5-11, part of the call of Jesus. Yet we cannot keep our children from all difficulties, and it would not even be good to do so. What we can do is walk with them through the tribulations that come their way so they can learn how to trust God in the midst of difficulty.

Jesus spent three years with his disciples, walking with these grown men through every possible situation in life so they could learn how to trust the Father as he trusted him. They saw him persecuted and accused by the Pharisees and the religious leaders. They saw him cursed at and accused by demons that possessed people along his path. They saw him work until he was utterly exhausted and yet still remain gracious and compassionate. Most powerful of all, they observed his quiet trust before God when his accusers threatened him and then crucified him. First Peter 2:23-24 tells us that "while being reviled, He did not revile in return; while suffering, He uttered no threats, but kept entrusting Himself to Him who judges righteously; and He Himself bore our sins in His body on the cross, so that we might die to sin and live to righteousness; for by His wounds you were healed."

If Jesus left a legacy of suffering to his disciples, all of whom died and suffered for the sake of his kingdom, then we must help our children understand this while they are in our homes. This will keep them from questioning their own difficulties when they are adults. If they know that in this world they will have tribulation and understand how to respond, they will be prepared to walk through their difficulties by faith. By showing our children how and when to "turn the other cheek" and helping them understand that being rejected is part of the cost of discipleship, we are really training them for victorious Christian living.

It is not just enough to *tell* our children these things though. We must respond to our own tribulations, difficulties, struggles, and stresses in a way that gives them a pattern to follow. We also see this as a lesson Peter learned from his relationship with Christ. In 1 Peter 2:19-21, Peter commends Christ as a model to those under his care:

> For this finds favor, if for the sake of conscience toward God a person bears up under sorrows when suffering unjustly. For

what credit is there if, when you sin and are harshly treated, you endure it with patience? But if when you do what is right and suffer for it you patiently endure it, this finds favor with God. For you have been called for this purpose, since Christ also suffered for you, leaving you an example for you to follow in His steps.

Keeping this reality in mind has helped Clay and me a lot when we have endured painful situations in our own Christian walk. One of the greatest surprises I faced when I went overseas to be a missionary was the critical and unloving attitudes of some of the missionaries I encountered. And as I look back on my almost thirty years in full-time Christian work, I see many situations in which our family has been criticized for our convictions, wrongly accused and judged for attitudes we never had, as well as simply gossiped about. We have had some of the people who we thought were quite committed to us turn their backs on us. This has caused great hurt and bitterness in the lives of our children.

"We have done so much for these people!" they protest. "We have had them in our home, loved them, helped them, given them gifts. How could real Christians do this?"

But little by little, as we have walked alongside our children in these situations to help them learn by our training and example, we have all come to understand that disappointment and betrayal are sometimes simply the cost of reaching out to people. It's not really so much a matter of "How can real Christians do this?" but the reality that all of us, even mature Christians, will make devastating mistakes sometimes and offend others because of our own sinful hearts.

My husband coined a term for these hurtful people that has become part of our family lexicon. They are *IRPs*—or irrational people. So much of the time we have ended up saying, "There are lots of IRPs in the world who will not be fair, who will choose to hurt you or even seek to tear you down. And sometimes, we will even be IRPs in the lives of others! But part of our responsibility to them as Christians is to love them, just as Jesus said for us to love our enemies. It does no good to get bitter and react. Jesus will help you learn how to cover these situations with love; after all, Peter told us that 'love covers a multitude of sins'!" (1 Peter 4:8).

How I wish I had learned this principle many years ago. It might have kept me from stumbling quite as much or being devastated when I encountered hurtful people along the way. I certainly hope it can keep my children from some unnecessary pain. And that's really interesting when you think about it. When we help our children understand that it's *normal* for Christians to encounter tribulations and to undergo suffering for Jesus' sake, we actually help protect them from unnecessary bitterness and disappointment.

Training our children to pay the cost of discipleship is a true gift of love—a love that requires the best of their lives. As they face trials with the Lord's help, they will come to see themselves as a part of bringing Christ's light to the world.

This year I asked Joel if he could remember a time in his life when he learned what it meant to be persecuted for the sake of righteousness. His time in the boys' choir five years ago immediately came to his mind. "That's when I began to learn that life is not always fair, but I can make a choice to accept my circumstances as an opportunity to be faithful to Christ. I think that is the story you should tell the moms, because it is a time when I began to really grow in understanding my walk with the Lord."

I have often prayed that my children would become mature believers, but my mother-heart never wanted them to have pain. As I was praying about this, I realized that in order for someone to become a general, he has to make it through many battles. If I want my children to become "generals," so to speak, for God's kingdom, then I can't expect to shield them from life's battles. Yet, God has given Clay and me to them to help them through these years of "basic training." We are the officers who help them prepare for the spiritual battles they will face in their lives. As we help them understand the nature of the battle and teach them to use their weapons—prayer, the Word of God, faith, the guidance of the Holy Spirit—then they will, through the gift of training, be prepared to battle in life for the glory of God with confidence and grace.

–A MOTHER'S PRAYER–

Merciful God,
We need you always to be our comfort in the midst of so much stress
and so many trials. Help us remember that you discipline us in order
to help us—and so that we may share in your holiness. Give us and
our children strength to persevere by faith through our trials, trusting
always in your love. Keep our children from Satan's grasp and give
them tenacity to endure difficulties in their lives with grace. Let the
testimonies of our lives reflect our strong faith in you and your Son,
Jesus, that you may be glorified in all that we do.

Amen

For Study and Discussion

Giving Your Children the Gift of Training

1. The book of Proverbs was written to teach young people how to be wise and how to have godly character. Determine to read from the first four chapters of Proverbs each day for one month to your children. Ask them to make a list of the wise principles they hear as you go along. Memorize one verse together each week and say it aloud daily.

2. Write down what you think should be the primary goal of our instruction and training. Then read 1 Timothy 1:5. What does this verse say about the goal of our instruction? How does your stated goal compare with the one Paul expressed to Timothy? What changes, if any, do you need to make to your goals and daily responses in the light of this comparison?

3. Hebrews 12:11 basically admits that discipline is not fun; in the short term, it brings sorrow instead of joy. But what does it say is the long-term result of this process of discipline? Can you think of issues with your children where you tend to back off from discipline because the process is so uncomfortable? List two ways in which you will strengthen your approach to loving discipline this

month. Ask for God's help and perhaps enlist the help of a friend
to keep you accountable for this.

4. As training in prayer, study the Lord's Prayer with your children.
Go through every line and discuss what it means. Help them
memorize it. Then say the prayer together every morning or every
night before you go to bed.

5. Think of some times when you've had the urge to step into a situation that was difficult for your children and "fix" it for them. What
happened? What are some ways you can train your children to
cope with trouble in a godly, mature manner?

PART FIVE

The Gift of Service

From the beginning, God always desired for us to be a part of his work in creation. He gave us the world, in fact, as the domain where we could work and glorify him.

Even after the Fall, God continued to involve men and women in his ongoing efforts to redeem humanity. Through prophets and psalmists and leaders, he called us both to love him and show justice and charity to others.

And then came Jesus, who completed the work of redemption and recruited us specifically to serve God by loving others. Jesus' first response to all the lost and hurting and sinful people he encountered in this world was compassion, and he called his followers to see people in the same way. He wants us to be laborers in the harvest field of life. Empowered by his Spirit, we are to be his mouth, his hands, and his feet in the work of restoring men and women to a personal relationship with him.

Service leads us to share
God's love with the world.

Chapter 17

Compassionate Harvest—a Model for Service

An excited chattering broke forth from the gathered crowd as Jesus and his disciples left the warm hospitality of a friend's house to venture into the crowded, dusty city streets. Men, women, and children all craned their necks to catch a glimpse of the famous Teacher.

"I think that's him—that Jesus everyone is talking about!" a chubby, older Jewish woman said to her companion. "He's the one who healed that girl after everyone thought she died. Quick—let's go see what he looks like!"

"See over there!" cried another. "He's with all those men who follow him!"

"Move aside! I need to get through," commanded a man as he pushed his way past several bystanders. "My daughter is deaf. I need Jesus to touch her. Please move!"

"Hey!" called out someone else. "We've all got problems. You can wait your turn!"

The noise was nothing new for Jesus' disciples, but they had never quite gotten used to it either. The crowds of people who followed the little band of men could be obnoxious—loud and smelly and needy. Always there were the sick and the lame and the blind crying out for healing while their relatives pushed and shoved their way to the front of the crowd.

"Jesus of Nazareth, have mercy on us! Jesus, please stop! Heal my child! Touch my son!"

The anguished look in the eyes of these determined people was always the same. Pain born of years of suffering seemed to frame the faces of each who clamored for his attention. Sometimes the disciples felt they just couldn't stand any more. But Jesus—Jesus never turned away. No matter how late the hour, no matter how tiring the day, Jesus seemed to look on each face with fresh love, strength, and willingness to help. He even touched the lepers!

"Jesus had better be careful," Bartholomew had muttered to Philip as Jesus reached to heal yet another limping leper. "Doesn't he realize leprosy is contagious? There's a *reason* they have to live away from everyone else!"

They didn't say anything to Jesus, of course. Almost nobody except the Pharisees was questioning Jesus these days. Even the swaggering, proud Romans who disdained the cluster of noisy and crowding Jewish people seemed to give this rabbi some slack. Why, hadn't one of the officers seen his servant healed by this incredible man?

But Jesus' main interest was not the Romans or the quarrelsome Pharisees or even the hundreds of ordinary Jews who followed him around. Instead, his attention seemed drawn to prostitutes, tax collectors, even Samaritans—the lowest of the low. Instead of wearing an attitude of disgust and disdain toward these social rejects, he spoke to them with genuine esteem and gentle love.

As many times as they saw it, the disciples were always perplexed. They wanted to follow their Lord, but they found it hard to understand him. Jesus seemed to be guided by an invisible force that kept him going long after their own reserves of energy were exhausted. On many days, they felt it push rudely against their own limits.

"Lord, we have to get some rest!" they would plead with him, for their feet were sore with walking, their bellies empty and rumbling, their patience tested beyond reason. "Can't we send the people away?" Still Jesus went on proclaiming the gospel of the kingdom and healing every kind of disease and every kind of despair.

The disciples were often confused as well as weary. Hadn't they left their places of business and their homes to follow after the Messiah? They had expected to see him bring to power the kingdom of the Jews that Isaiah had foretold. Instead, they seemed to have given up the comfort of a regular life to spend their days with invalids, outcasts, women, and children.

Yet as impatient as the disciples sometimes grew, they wouldn't have missed being with Jesus while he ministered to the multitudes. To see blind men regain their vision, a desperately ill child healed to run and skip, demons desert a possessed man when cast into a herd of pigs—who could ever forget such experiences? Why, Jesus had even commanded the sea, just as God had commanded the sea in the days of Moses. His words carried such authority, and the disciples couldn't help feeling they were going to be part of something big. Something world changing. They had been the agents of his miracles themselves as they passed out bread and fish to the thousands or healed people in his name.

On this afternoon, however, the disciples somehow managed to get

Jesus away from the pressing crowds. They had made their way out of the city and down the road to a new town, only to wait for an hour in the hot sun along with crowds of people traveling toward Nazareth. An ox had fallen and overturned a large cart, casting all the bags of grain over the road. Jesus had stopped to help the pitiful man, who had lost control of his aged animal. But then he had led the disciples up a hillside where they could rest under the shade of a twisted old tree—a welcome reprieve from the jostles and smells of the crowded lane.

What a relief! The disciples munched on stalks of fresh wheat picked from the nearby fields as they rested on the ground, enjoying the shade. But Jesus seemed to be gazing back down toward the road. The disciples followed his gaze and could detect nothing of special interest. But Jesus' eyes were wistful, filled with as much longing as the eyes of a mother whose firstborn child had been given to the service of the Romans.

"What are you looking at, Master?" said Thomas with his customary frankness. "There is no one in particular who awaits us."

But Jesus was seeing the multitudes of people he had recently touched on their wearisome journey. His heart was filled with compassion as he remembered how they looked—distressed and downcast and confused, like sheep without a shepherd. Turning his eyes toward the disciples, he earnestly spoke to them from a heavy heart:

"The harvest is plentiful, but the workers are few. Therefore beseech the Lord of the harvest to send out workers into his harvest."

And then, for the first time, they truly understood—his moods and his thoughts and why he was here in the first place. Why hadn't they seen it all along? They had heard about him standing before the whole congregation of people in Nazareth and reading from the scroll of Isaiah, "The Spirit of the Lord is upon me, because he anointed me to preach the gospel to the poor. He has sent me to proclaim release to the captives, and recovery of sight to the blind, to set free those who are oppressed, to proclaim the favorable year of the Lord."

Jesus indeed was fulfilling prophecy before their eyes. He reached out to people not because they deserved his healing, restoring, and forgiving touch but because love had brought him here in the first place. Loving compassion—the heart of the Father lived out through the work of his beloved Son—was what gave his feet and hands and voice strength to reach out to so many.

Now, the disciples realized, he was calling them on this mission of compassion, this service of mercy and love. This is what he had meant when he first called them to be fishers of men. Their mission was not to set up kingdoms of power on this earth but to live out the redemptive kindness of God in service to the needy and the downtrodden. This service of love is what would turn the world upside down. It was all beginning to make sense.

"Well, Lord," said Thomas as he got to his feet and brushed off his robe. "Isn't it time we got back on the road? We all have some work to do."[1]

Giving our children the gift of service is not really a matter of teaching them what to do. It's more a matter of helping them look at other people through Jesus' eyes and respond as he did. It really is that simple—though it's often not easy.

Jesus looked into the hearts of people and focused on their real needs. In a prostitute he saw the need for forgiveness, in the children a need for affection and time, in Nicodemus a searching heart. But Jesus did more than just recognize these needs; he was also compelled by compassion to reach out in his power and to meet the needs of those he encountered. He ministered with a heart of love and with willing hands, and he called his followers to the same kind of service.

Jesus' heart of love and his allegiance to his loving Father was so great, in fact, that he was willing to give up his own greatness and put the needs of others above his own. Paul wrote in Philippians 2:7 that he "emptied Himself" and took the form of a "bond-servant," making himself available in loving, humble service to all those people God placed in his path.

This model for ministry, unfortunately, is one that easily gets pushed aside in favor of more glamorous kinds of "Christian service." In the world of evangelical Christianity, where "strategic ministry" is a common catch phrase and "moving with the movers" is often held up as a principle of leadership, we need to be careful that we don't become like the Pharisees. They were informed and educated men but useless to the cause of Christ precisely because they lacked compassion and humility. They were sure of their religious practices and probably knew exactly what their "philosophy of ministry" was. Yet Jesus described them as a brood of vipers—the very worst kind of snakes—because they had let loving service be eclipsed by religiosity.

I have been a believer many years, yet I don't always practice Jesus' principle of serving in love as well as I should. I have, however, come to terms with the fact that the ministry Jesus calls me to is rarely convenient. People who need me never seem to wait until I am fully rested and organized and ready to help them. Instead, their needs always seem to intrude into my already busy life. And what people want from me is almost never what I think of as "important" ministry. I want to give them pearls of wisdom, and they want me to pick them up when their car has died or cry with them over a problem at home.

The ministry of motherhood with my children, especially, can sometimes seem extremely nonstrategic. Settling fusses between immature boys who are fighting over whose turn it is on the computer does not seem like a vital form of ministry, and yet it is in such everyday situations that our children learn vital relational skills. Comforting wailing babies, tending to sick children, cleaning up messes, prevailing upon teenagers to do assigned chores—all standard mothering tasks—can seem depressingly mundane. Yet when I study the ministry of Christ, I see that he responded in compassion to whatever need was presented to him, not just those needs that seemed "worthy" or important.

I'm not the first person to observe that the impact of Christianity on our culture has decreased over the course of the past century. The media have been infiltrated with degenerate values learned from people who make immoral choices. Divorce has become as common among Christians as nonbelievers. Wickedness has been accepted at the highest level of leadership, where scandals are commonplace. And of course the reasons for these developments are complicated and many. Yet I can't help but think that one reason Christianity has lost influence is that Christians have not found it convenient to respond to real needs the way Jesus did—ministering to real people, teaching God's Word, and serving people humbly and lovingly.

Christians have made every excuse for not going into the harvest fields, and the Christian cause has suffered as a result. Yet Christ's words about the harvest's being plentiful hold true even in our time.

Service always carries a cost—in time, energy, material possessions, reputation, or effort. Yet if we fail to lead in serving others, our whole Christian testimony will be null and void.

What good does it do to sit through a sermon at church about the needs of "unchurched" people to hear the gospel, to discuss in the car on the way home what a good sermon it was, but then never stop to talk to the family down the street who obviously sleeps in every Sunday?

What good does it do to piously read the Sermon on the Mount but never reach out to feed the hungry (perhaps with a hamburger dinner for the homeless guy by the underpass) or clothe the naked (a "Coats for Kids" project) or visit the imprisoned (volunteering for a prison ministry)?

And what good are all our efforts at raising children who love the Lord if we stop short of sending them out from our homes to bring God's redemptive love to those who need it? Giving our children the gift of service means not just telling them that service is important but actually taking them with us and showing them *how* to serve.

I believe Jesus will hold each of us responsible for the stewardship of the good news he has given us. If we are to succeed in our calling of raising children with hearts for God, then we must see ourselves responsible for all of those who are like sheep without a shepherd. We must involve our family deeply in meeting needs if our children are ever going to understand that they were created to serve God by serving others.

When Jesus asked the disciples to "follow Me," he was asking for each man's entire life—time, allegiance, talents, and will. Surely he requires no less from us or from our children. We read in Ephesians 2:10 that "we are [God's] workmanship, created in Christ Jesus for good works, which God prepared beforehand so that we should walk in them." To me, this indicates that God has set aside specific tasks for each of us to do, according to our personalities, skills, and circumstances, to further his kingdom. Is it possible that there are people in our everyday lives whose needs are going unmet because we have neglected to do the loving work the Lord has set aside just for us?

May God open our eyes and our hearts, then, that we may say yes to his call to compassionate service. And as we obey him in reaching out to others, may our children come to see themselves as those who will drop their nets to follow Jesus wherever he leads—and then, at the Spirit's prompting, let down their nets to become fishers of men.

Chapter 18

Serving with
a Willing Heart

"Mom, I don't want to go help out at this church. Please don't make us go! I don't know anyone there, and I won't know what to do! I was looking forward to a nice, relaxed day at home!" Thirteen-year-old Nathan pleaded for a lost cause as we all piled into the car.

The Christmas season had always provided lots of opportunities for us as a family to celebrate the season and reach out to others in interesting ways. Christmas open houses in our home had given us great opportunities to get to know our neighbors. Filling Christmas boxes with toiletries and sweet surprises for kids at a homeless shelter had helped build friendships and camaraderie in a youth group. Caroling at our local retirement center and serving cake to the residents had not only brightened the day of some lonely older adults but also given our children a gratifying sense of being useful. Christmas musical programs and concerts had built cherished memories. Every year, in fact, had brought us a myriad of opportunities to celebrate the season by reaching out and also to celebrate our relationships with other Christians.

But this year was different! December was here, and we didn't even have a home church, much less a slew of invitations for any Christmas parties with friends. We felt alone and desolate, and the "Bah, humbug" attitude was pervasive in our home. None felt the least inclination to reach out! It was one of those times when I questioned if the Lord really meant for us to move so often with the demands of our ministry. Perhaps this had been one move too many, I thought as I faced a lonely holiday that threatened to be just like all the other lonely days we had recently spent together.

But then a friend had called and told me about an opportunity to help with a community project in which toys were collected and passed out to needy families. I thought maybe my boys would catch the Christmas spirit as they helped out at this big event. So I had arranged for them to go, even though they insisted they didn't want to. I knew my boys had big hearts, but I also knew they dreaded the prospect of going to one more new place without the familiarity of friends. As they grumpily climbed into the car, I whispered a prayer that the Lord would somehow redeem the time and improve their attitudes.

Later in the day, Sarah drove to pick up the boys. I was making dinner when Nathan burst through the front door and, in his typical extroverted way, announced that he was home. As I went to greet him, his face was lit with a smile that filled the whole room.

"Mom, I can't wait to tell you about the day! It was so much fun, and I wish we could go back!"

The story began to pour forth in quick words. It seemed that the adults had needed the bigger boys in one place to carry out loads of toys to the cars of moms who were getting gifts for their children. That was Joel's job. So Nathan had been relegated to the basement, where he was asked to take care of the children while their moms picked up packages.

Now, baby-sitting isn't a high-status job to most young men. However, Nathan was immediately drawn to help the kids, especially when he saw how needy their families seemed to be. As he attempted to keep the little ones settled in a small room, the Lord brought an idea to his mind. He found a little piece of blue play-clay, rolled it up in his hand, and said, "Hmmm, I think I see something in your ear!" Quick as a wink, he reached out and pulled the blue clay out of a delighted child's ear.

"Wow, how did you do that? Do it again! Can you pull some out of my pocket?"

Again with a flourish he "magically" pulled the clay out of another child's pocket.

Within minutes all the little ones crowded around him and were yelling out simultaneously, "Do it to me! Pull it out of my head!" (or mouth or pants or jacket or nose).

With his skills as a budding magician who had practiced hours of sleight-of-hand tricks, Nathan was able to delight the children, give some of his love away, and come home refreshed with the knowledge that something he loved to do was useful in God's hands.

"Mom, you know I've always had so much fun doing magic, but today I saw how God could use my skills at magic to help me reach out to kids. I felt so good helping those people. I wish we could go back tomorrow! I'm actually glad you made us go!"

Training our children to put their energies and talents to work in the area of ministry is so important. We must not just tell our children that people should share their faith and then do nothing; we must show them a life in which we are sharing our own faith. We must not just talk about the need for more people to give to the poor; we must involve our children with us as we pray about where to give our money. And sometimes, I believe, we must gently push them beyond what is comfortable and natural so they learn to rely on the Lord's supernatural power as they seek to serve.

Two equal heartbeats are involved in training our children to serve. The first heartbeat is helping them learn to really see the needs of people they encounter on a daily basis, just as Jesus did. This is partly a matter of taking the time to really pay attention to people, partly a matter of learning to respond to the Holy Spirit's nudgings. If we ask for and are sensitive to the Spirit's work in our lives, he will help us be aware of what people need most and how we can help.

But the second heartbeat is helping our children develop a willingness to take the initiative and act. This means they may need to overcome feelings of shyness, inadequacy, and laziness. It may mean actually setting aside time in a busy schedule to help others. It definitely means learning to reach past their natural inclinations and to serve whether or not they feel like serving.

Giving our children the gift of service, in other words, may well mean interfering with their natural, sinful, or just immature self. Nathan really didn't want to go help out with the Christmas campaign, though afterward he was glad he did.

I have often said to my children, "It is *natural* to be selfish or self-absorbed. Everybody is naturally like that. It is *supernatural* to see the needs and desires of others and seek their best through your actions. As you mature, and as you get to know the Lord better and love him, you will begin to be more concerned about others and their lives."

I don't have any desire to make my children feel guilty for what they are naturally—sinful and immature. But I do want to lead them away from their natural sinful tendencies, to show them how to use self-control and discipline their character, how to walk with God and let him develop in them a heart of compassion. And I have found that I as a mom can facilitate this process by giving my children an occasional push in the direction of ministry. I ask God for help in finding activities that will fit my children's abilities and whet their appetites for service. And then, sometimes, I need to hold the line. I need to make sure they serve, even when I know their hearts aren't in it, trusting that the Lord will work on their hearts to make them more willing.

Jesus did exactly that with his disciples when the mothers brought their children to be blessed by him. The disciples, remember, rebuked the little ones; they just weren't interested in children's ministries! When Jesus saw this, however, "He was indignant and said to them, 'Permit the children to come to Me; do not hinder them; for the kingdom of God belongs to such as these.... And He took them in His arms and began blessing them, laying His hands on them" (Mark 10:14-16).

Jesus didn't hesitate to interfere with his disciples' natural desires when it came to ministry. He corrected them, instructed them, and showed them how to minister in the context of everyday life. He gave them what they needed, not what they thought they wanted. As a mother who is a follower of Christ, I believe I am called to do the same with my children.

As I have prayed about this over the years, I see the same pattern in the Bible as I observe in people today—that is, sin in our lives makes us resist responsibility. When the twelve Jewish spies went into the Promised Land to see what God had planned to provide in the way of blessing, ten of the leaders saw there were giants in the land and grew defeated in their hearts. They were certain that the Hebrews were too small and too weak to occupy the new territory (as though God didn't *know* the giants were there and hadn't already planned to defeat them). Later, when the Israelite army came up against Goliath, everyone assumed the huge man couldn't be defeated, and he couldn't—until a boy named David chose to rely on God instead of common wisdom. Even the disciples, as we have seen throughout this book, tended to follow their own natural inclination instead of heeding Jesus' training.

Throughout the Bible, we see that there was always plenty of work for God's people to do, but not always enough workers who were willing to reach out and do the Father's will with the help of the Holy Spirit. I believe the same is true today, and I pray that my life and my children's lives can help reverse the trend. I don't want to raise children who hear Christ's call and then dream up excuses for not following him!

In Luke 9:57-62, Jesus gave three examples of those who did just that—people who said they wanted to follow Jesus but then gave excuses about why they had to put it off.

The first said, "I will follow you wherever you go!" Jesus' reply was that "the Son of man has nowhere to lay His head," implying that he knew the man wasn't serious about "wherever."

The next person said, "Permit me first to go and bury my father"—in other words, "When my parents are gone and I'm released from more important responsibilities, I will follow you." But Jesus wasn't buying that excuse. He said, "Allow the dead to bury their own dead; but as for you, go and proclaim everywhere the kingdom of God."

The third person said, "I will follow You, Lord; but first permit me to say good-bye to those at home." And Jesus' astute answer this time was, "No one, after putting his hand to the plow and looking back, is fit for the kingdom of God."

Jesus wasn't looking for excuses from his followers. What he wanted from them was total commitment; he wanted them to be available to minister at any moment. Even the night before he died, he prayed these words in his High Priestly prayer; "As You sent Me into the world, I also have sent them into the world" (John 17:18). His most pressing concern, growing out of his compassionate heart, was sending out workers for his kingdom—people who were willing to seek and save the lost and to minister to their needs.

As I have become committed to Jesus Christ as Lord over all areas, I have learned to be more and more sensitive to the prompting of his Spirit when I see the needs of others around me in my life. I am quick to reach out to help, since I know that in this life, I am his hands, his voice, his comfort, his forgiveness to a dying world. I am trying, more and more, to follow the words of Daniel: "The people who know their God will display strength and take action" (Daniel 11:32).

In the process, I am becoming more aware that effective and loving service is less a matter of qualifications and more a matter of willingness. Many leaders, speakers, and writers have become well known in Christian leadership, not because of unique skills or spiritual strength, but because they obeyed the Lord by being faithful to commit themselves to a life of ministry. One small step led to another and to another until they had much responsibility in the Lord's work.

The disciples, remember, were completely unqualified for ministry. They were certainly untrained as religious leaders. But as they committed themselves to Christ and trusted him to push them past their natural limitations toward his supernatural love, they became effective ministers of his gospel. Their authority came from Christ, from loving him and obeying him and following him.

If my goal is to send my children into a life of fruitful ministry, then I must pass on the vision of ministry—that God does want to use their lives. I must lead my children in ministry, showing them how to see needs and meet needs. I must also provide the opportunities of ministry, so that as they mature in Christ, they will see themselves as personally responsible to be about his work in the lives of other people. Most of all, I must do whatever I can to help them develop a willing heart, even if it means giving them a little push to help them past their natural hesitation. This, I believe, is what it means to give them the gift of service.

—A MOTHER'S PRAYER—

Compassionate Lord,
Help us each day to see others with eyes of compassion and mercy.
Make us and our children willing to take the time and opportunity
to reach out in your redemptive love to those in our lives who need to
know you. Help all of us in our families be salt and light to those
who live in darkness. Give our children hearts that are open to serve
you by serving others. Together and individually, may we go into the
world to serve you and your kingdom purposes.

Amen

Chapter 19

Serving with
Hardworking Hands

Dreariness seemed to invade our home and permeate its atmosphere as we all looked out at the cold winter day. Zero-degree weather is almost unheard of in Nashville, and yet we had had frigid days for almost a week. The forlorn-looking trees were barren of leaves, the grass yellow and dry, the clouds and sky gray and dark. To top it all off, three of my children were battling a respiratory sort of flu with coughing, wheezing, and low-grade fevers. I was beginning to have the chills and knew that my own illness would be following on the heels of theirs.

"Mommy, can you think of something fun?" Joy asked quietly. "Remember when we used to make forts in your big closet? Do you think you could help me build one today? I'll surprise Nathan and the kids. I'll make them get-well cards and a snack. I want them to have fun and feel better, since we haven't gotten to play in several days." In our last home, we'd had a large, walk-in closet in our room where we would drape sheets to form a tent and then set up a small TV-VCR and pallets on the floor. Now, in our new house, Joy had a large closet and was eager to recreate that fun experience.

"Sure, sweetie," I told her. "I think that is a great idea. I'm glad you want to surprise your brothers and sister and encourage them. I'll help you in just a few minutes."

It sounded like such a good, simple idea. We were both excited to jump into our tent building.

But when I joined Joy downstairs in her bedroom, I was surprised at what I saw when I opened her door. Clothes were strewn all over the bed and floor. Little pieces of paper, scissors, glue, and colored markers gave evidence of creativity at work—messy creativity. A food tray sat near her pillow with dried-up juice residue on a favorite cup, cracker crumbs, and a dirty plate. Doll clothes and dolls sat in a disordered circle all their own. A knocked-over pile of clean laundry indicated that someone had been rummaging through to find needed socks or underwear before putting the clothes away, but at least it was near the dresser.

It was then I realized that the illness of the past few days had really taken its toll on me. Joy's room was proof that I was completely out of touch with what had been taking place in her life.

"It looks like you have a lot of work to do before we can build a fort in the closet, Joy. I'll help you, and I don't think it will take too long."

I tried to encourage her as her face fell from the realization of what she needed to do before we could begin her fun project. It had all sounded so easy a few minutes before, but often great ideas require a lot of sweat equity to develop into reality.

Joy carried the food tray to the kitchen. I gathered up the dirty clothes and placed them in the hamper. She picked up clothes that had fallen down in her closet and put them on hangers. I threw away the scraps of papers and stowed the other craft supplies. She put her dolls away and packed their clothes in a little trunk. I cleared out discarded Christmas presents from the back of the closet. She ran to look for the vacuum cleaner so we could clean the area of crumbs before putting down a blanket. I rummaged around in the basement to find a little table for her fort so she could color and draw in her books. We moved her CD player with her favorite stories and music so she could listen in her little haven. We piled up pillows and spread out the blanket so it could all be as comfy as possible.

As we finally finished an hour and a half later, Joy looked at her watch and sat down on her pillows in a huff.

"You know, Mommy, when I thought about having a neat fort to play in and do some nice things for the kids, I thought it was a great idea, but I didn't count on all the work we would have to do! Working takes more time than you would ever think. I'm almost too tired to play!"

Most worthwhile endeavors—whether they involve housework and chores, schoolwork, serving outside the home or providing hospitality within it, or training our children to be servants of the Lord—end up taking more time, energy, effort, and character than we ever thought they would. Joy learned that in her tent-building adventure. I've had to learn it again and again in my daily life. And I've certainly found it true when it comes to my attempts to serve God and others. It's one thing to get excited by an inspiring sermon on reaching the world for Christ. It's an altogether different experience to meet the requirements of real, live, sinful, and needy human beings, especially my own children!

When Clay and I first decided to start a family, I read a lot of books about parenting. I got excited about the idea of training and loving my

197

children into obedient, godly young people. I didn't understand that doing that would take years of work involving daily instruction and correction, reassurance and encouragement, not to mention the endless cycle of lessons, dishwashing, laundry, and meals. I can honestly say that raising children is one of the most wonderful experience I have ever had—and the hardest work I have ever done.

So I tend to smile a little when I hear my children talk about their big dreams. I know they have a taste of what is ahead because they have been involved in our ministry for many years. But still their idealism leads them to think it will somehow be different for them.

"Mom," they may say, "Eric Liddell's biography is so inspiring; I want to do something wonderful like he did!" But when it comes to washing dishes or helping a younger sibling clean her room or taking time to minister to the needs of an older woman who needs someone to read to her, it's a different story. "I want to do something important that will really change the world! Not just the little stuff!" is the complaint I sometimes hear.

The heart is willing, in other words, but the flesh is weak.

As we look to the lives of the disciples, we see many instances in which they were eager to follow Jesus into ministry but then stubbed their toes against the mundane realities of ministry. They hungered for great things but then failed to live up to their own expectations even in small matters.

The night before Jesus was crucified, he spent hours talking intimately to his disciples as friends before he was to leave them. We read that after singing a hymn together at the close of the evening of the Passover supper, Jesus and his disciples walked to one of their favorite places, the Mount of Olives. There, in the cool darkness of the evening, Jesus sat down with his friends and continued telling them what would happen to them that very night. Matthew 26:31-46 tells some of what took place.

Jesus told his disciples that all of them would "fall away" from him that evening. Peter immediately answered him and said, "Even though all may fall away because of You, I will never fall away."

I believe that Peter sincerely, with his whole heart, meant to be faithful to Jesus. But Peter was insensitive to his own vulnerability and weakness. It is at this time that Jesus told him he would deny him three times.

Peter again said, "Even if I have to die with You, I will not deny You." And of course we know how well he kept that promise!

A little later Jesus asked Peter and the other disciples to sit with him while he prayed. He didn't ask them to pray with him or to do anything but stay awake and keep him company. But they couldn't keep their eyes open. When Jesus found them sleeping, he shook them awake and exhorted them to "keep watching and praying that you may not enter into temptation." But he also acknowledged that "the spirit is willing, but the flesh is weak."

Again, the disciples desired to do what Jesus asked. They knew what he was facing—he had told them very clearly—and they wanted to be there for him. But as soon as Jesus left them, they fell asleep. They just couldn't help it. It was evening, and they had already talked with Jesus most of the night. Their stomachs were full from the Passover meal. Having gone through the triumphal entry with him that very week, traveled with him throughout Jerusalem, and spent an emotional evening with him, they were tired beyond measure. Their exhaustion overwhelmed their best intentions at the most crucial moment in history.

Then Judas came, and the disciples' worst fears were realized. Jesus was taken away to be tried, and they all ran away in fear, fulfilling the words he had spoken to them that very night. They had failed in doing what the Lord had asked. They had let him down, and the bitterness of failure must have stuck in their throats.

I know a little about how that feels. In my experience, serving the Lord has always required more of me than I expected. I tend to be a passionate, visionary person. I love the idea of changing the world, but I tend to get overwhelmed by the details of daily life. My spirit has usually been willing, but my flesh has often been weak.

As I have matured over the years, however, I have learned a lot about failure, perseverance, and hard work. I've learned to look ahead, to count the cost of ministry. (I believe I would have struggled so much less in my marriage, my parenting, and my ministry, if I had better assessed the work involved in what I wanted to do.) More important, I've also learned from Jesus and Peter that even we passionate, visionary types can live past our failures and disappointment and actually get the important work done. It has been a long road of growing maturity over many years of seemingly unnoticed faithfulness. But now I look back and see God's integrity in my life as I reflect on the ways he used me and stretched my faith and built my character. Sometimes he required more of me than I thought I was capable of giving, but he gave me more than I could ever have dreamed.

If we are doing the Lord's work, we can know our efforts are not in vain. Whether we are building a tent for the neighborhood children, cooking a tasty meal for a sick neighbor, or serving our own sick child with a tray of appealing goodies, we are teaching our children what it means to serve with hardworking hands.

At the same time, I think we can help our children prepare for their own lives of service by helping them understand what service really means. And we can help them learn to follow through and persevere until they see the fruitful product of their labor. In practical terms, this means we hold our children responsible for doing their work and serving others from the time they are small. As they clean their rooms and do their chores and help entertain guests, we check their progress, send them back to complete unfinished tasks. Sometimes we work alongside our children when they grow discouraged—as I did with Joy in her room—but we also resist the temptation just to do it for them. When they fail or fall behind, we comfort and remind them how God handles our "fleshly" weakness, then urge them to try again.

As our children hear our words of instruction to reach out humbly to others in need and as we discipline them to persevere and do things right, they will learn a pattern of hard work that will enhance their witness and bring stability to their lives. And yet it will be in the example of our own persevering faithfulness, patience, and trust in the Lord that our children will learn to do the work of compassionate servants.

Just this week as I was working on this manuscript, I have watched Sarah serve our family with generous love and creativity. As my deadline hovered, with constant pressure over my head, she volunteered to help me out. While I was writing, she read a book to Joy. She purchased a favorite gift for one of her brothers and left it on his bed as a surprise with an "I believe in you" note. She drove to the store when we were out of milk and eggs. And then on Monday afternoon, when I emerged bug-eyed from staring at my computer, I found her busy in the kitchen making a fresh Greek salad with grilled chicken, red onions, and feta cheese. She had set the table and lit the candles and turned on music for our feast.

"Sarah, I don't deserve a child like you. You are absolutely wonderful! The finest of fine! I know this week has been a lot of work. I appreciate you more than you will ever know!"

"But, Mom, it's not more than you have done for me a thousand times. It was in our home that I learned all that I know."

What a gift of encouragement it was to me to see the fruit of maturity in my daughter's life. I had planted many seeds of service in her heart over the years. And God had honored my willing spirit and my efforts to train my daughter and brought the seeds to fruition, giving her a desire and an ability to serve. Even as I was learning to persevere in serving God by attending to the work of serving my family, Sarah was learning to serve as well.

And that, after all, is my goal for all my children. As I strive to give them the gift of service, I pray that their loving hearts and hardworking hands will be a blessing to others for the rest of their lives.

—A MOTHER'S PRAYER—

Sweet Jesus,
Help us learn from your example how to persist in the hard work of
ministry. It cost you everything to serve through the love of the Father,
and yet you will be exalted in heaven through all eternity. Help us
train our children, even as we keep learning, how to labor for the
sakes of others with joy and diligence. Let them develop integrity in
their lives that they might be true to your call to them. Let excellence
be the standard with which they accomplish all the works you have
for them to do.

Amen

Chapter 20

Serving in God's Strength

Every January, as we tuck the holiday season behind us with all its memories and events, my children turn their hearts with excitement toward another memorable event—the WholeHearted Mother conference in Dallas. This annual conference put on by our ministry has been a part of their lives almost as long as they can remember. We started when Joy was just a few months old and her brothers and sisters were gap-toothed elementary-age kids. Now Joy is nine, the others are well into their teens, and the conference has become an important annual milestone for all of us.

Each year the ballroom at the Harvey Hotel is filled to capacity—almost a thousand women attending from thirty different states and four foreign countries, and no room for even one more mom. We love these women, and they love us back. The little army of blue-shirted volunteers who help the conference run smoothly—dads, moms, and kids of all ages—have become like a family to all of us, so each conference feels like a reunion. And because we always want the children to be involved in what we are doing, our four and the children of our board members have always played an integral role in our conference ministry.

As our children matured, we have always wanted them to learn to be comfortable in front of crowds. A part of our "training" plan has been to give them experience at all sorts of ministry situations as they grew up, regardless of personality or skill. Our hope was that our children would grow up naturally with the idea of ministry, thinking of themselves as people who were designed to reach out to others. Then, when they were older, they would be experienced and confident in serving others and able to respond to the needs of those God put in their lives. That was the idea anyway. So from the beginning, we have brought our children on stage with us to help lead the actual conferences.

Little Joy, for instance, has always opened our WholeHearted Mother conferences with her own speech welcoming the moms. Sarah, who has been singing with Clay all her life, eventually became the pianist for the worship team. In past years she also told about books that influenced her life and even presented some dramatic readings from her first published book. Joel, my quiet, reserved second child, once wielded a heavy, shining silver Knight Templar sword that his dad had presented him on his thirteenth birthday. Much to his surprise, his heartfelt speech about the sword and its meaning was met with a standing ovation. And Nathan, our natural performer and extroverted entertainer, was always in his element at conferences. After years of bantering with the crowd and telling them of our vacation adventures, he finally moved on to more auspicious performances, performing some of his "gospel magic" for the whole crowd.

Our children's contributions to our conferences have become a treasured tradition to us. But this year, as January rolled around again, we realized we might need to reevaluate. Now that our older ones are no longer "cute little kids," they really needed to perform at a more adult level, and we wanted to make sure they still wanted to be involved. So as we sat together one Sunday evening eating pizza, Clay asked them what they wanted to do this year.

Nathan, as usual, dived right in: "I really want to have a chance to do another act from my new magic show. Maybe this year I can introduce Michael"—his former next-door neighbor and best friend—"as my partner. I bet some of their kids would like to learn magic tricks as a hobby. I can tell the moms how I got involved."

Sarah was feeling more reticent: "I have been so much in the limelight the past couple of years with my new book that I think I will just sit back this year and play the piano." That was fine with us.

Joy, who had been learning American Sign Language, couldn't decide if she wanted to sign along with one of the worship songs or just stick with greeting the moms. We told her there was plenty of time to make up her mind.

But Joel, meanwhile, seemed to be brooding in the corner, a worried look on this face. My lanky, six-foot-three older son has been taking acoustic guitar lessons for several years and was beginning to catch up with his guitar-playing dad. He loved music and even dreamed of doing something professional with it someday. He had joined Sarah and Clay the year before to complete a little worship ensemble for the conference, and we expected he would want to do that again. But we soon learned there was more on his mind.

"Mom and Dad," he said, "I have a song I'd like to try to sing, but what if I blow it? I really want to do some music for the weekend, and I don't just want to play the guitar with Sarah and you, Dad. But I—I've just never done anything like that before!"

We encouraged him to try the song in front of us. He got his guitar out and started in on a beautiful song I had heard him do perfectly in his room many times before. But his voice sounded a little strained. He had a hard time hitting some of the notes. The final blow was forgetting the words and having to stop in the middle. He thumped the guitar in frustration. "I'll get it," he said. "I'm just nervous. I—"

"Look, Joel," Clay said gently. "It's no big deal to us. It might be that performing in front of lots of people doesn't suit your personality now that you are older. Please don't feel any pressure. You don't have to do the song if you're not ready."

After Joel left the room, Clay confessed to me that he had greatly embarrassed himself when he was a young performer because he didn't have enough experience. "I want Joel to perform when he is ready, but not until then. I want him to feel a sense of competence."

And so we left it alone.

A couple of days later, Joel came into my room in a state of agitation. "Do you think I should do a song, Mom?" It was as though something inside of him was driving this struggle.

"We are going to leave this one up to you, honey. What do you want me to say?" I asked, trying to figure out what was really bothering him.

Then he told me he had been reading the biography of Keith Green, a young musician who died in an airplane crash in the early 1980s. The powerful story had stimulated in Joel a desire to really do something with his life. Youthful passion for the Lord was beginning to surge through his heart, and he really wanted to communicate that through his music. But the thought of performing alone in front of so many was daunting. "I really don't know what to do, Mom. I don't want to let anybody down."

I assured him that the Lord would work in his time to give him an answer. "Why don't you pray about it?" was my closing advice.

Two days later Joel came in again, but this time his face seemed at ease. He had been reading the Bible that morning, he said, and the Lord had spoken to his heart.

"You know, Mom, I'm kind of shy by nature and I don't feel my best in crowds. So I've been struggling between how I feel I am naturally and what I feel I want to do. Anyway, I was reading in Joshua 1, and God kept telling Joshua to be strong and courageous." He quoted verse 9 from memory: "'Do not tremble or be dismayed, for the LORD your God is with you wherever you go.' This really spoke to my heart, Mom. I think I am going to make it my life verse. I want my faith in God to help me be courageous."

"That's wonderful, honey," I said quietly. But Joel obviously had more on his mind.

"I really do feel that God wants me to do this song because of its message," he said. "I want to overcome my fear, to prove to myself that I can do what is in my heart, which is to tell others to make the most of every opportunity. So I've decided I'm going to sing 'Seize the Day' and tell people about the life of Keith Green. And I think I'll ask Sarah to sing harmony with me for moral support. Will you and Dad let me do it?"

I think you already know my answer to that question! How excited we were that Joel had come to this decision by his own conviction. The goal of all our instruction and training, after all, was for our children to develop their own mature walk with the Lord—hammering out their own convictions, fighting their own spiritual battles, and developing heartfelt testimonies of their own. That is exactly what we saw happen at our conference this year.

Joel and Sarah chose to sing "Seize the Day," a wonderful song written by Carolyn Arends, the opening night of our conference to introduce my talk on the mission of motherhood. Having my two older children share their testimony about how God had worked in their lives seemed a perfect introduction to my message.

When it was time for them to go on, I smiled at Joel and patted him on the back. "I know you will do well, Joel. Your heart will really minister to the moms. I will be praying for you." I said it confidently, but inside I was nervous and excited, pleading with God to help Joel and Sarah through the performance, wanting it to be a good experience for him and hoping my smile wouldn't betray my own nervous feelings. Singing in front of people had always been a challenge for me, so I couldn't help transferring my own past feelings into the situation. But my heart was so excited and proud of Joel's willingness to be used by God in this way.

Joel walked over to the microphone and appeared casual and confident. He shared the story of how his passion for the Lord had been ignited by the faithful testimony of a godly young man, Keith Green. Then he said, "I would like to close with a song that communicates what I have felt in my heart—that I want to seize the day and not waste any moment of my life. I want to live my life telling others about my Lord, and I want to encourage each of you to seize your days for his glory."

His guitar notes played out sweet and clear, and Sarah's and Joel's voices blended into a chorus that called all of us in the room before the throne of God to commit to his purposes. If he missed a note or forgot a word, I never noticed. I was just so thankful for the bridge of faith my son had crossed.

In the end, the measure of my success as a mother will not be how well I have taught my kids or cared for them but whether I have been faithful in helping them respond to God's call on their lives. Seeing my children develop a heart for God's service and begin to find their own place of ministry in the world is a reachable goal for me as a mother, because God has designed me to fulfill this purpose. This is the true ministry of motherhood—to usher my children into the living presence of God, to nurture in them a heart for Jesus and the Great Commission he has called each of us to fulfill.

Jesus isn't limited by the personalities of our children or by our own personalities or by our education or life skills or lack of the same. He is only limited by our trying to do his will our way, in our flesh. When he takes over, he confounds the limitations of our natural life circumstances. If we trust him, he will do whatever is necessary to accomplish his purposes in our lives, and he'll do it in his own time.

The disciple Peter, you may remember, was actually able to walk on water—as long as he kept his eyes on Jesus and trusted in the Lord's strength. "Lord, if it is You," he cried, "command me to come to You on the water" (Matthew 14:28).

And it happened! Peter didn't do it perfectly, of course. He lost sight of what he was doing and needed Jesus to rescue him from sinking. But his fundamental faith in Jesus and his desire to step out into the realm of miracles may be the very reason that Peter was called "the rock"—and this particular rock turned out to be unsinkable.

As we give our children the gift of service, we are to believe in what they will become and affirm them as they take their small steps of faith. More important, we must give them over to the Lord, trusting that he will be able to take them faithfully on this road to discipleship. After all, service was his plan for them from the beginning—just like grace and inspiration and faith and training. As we launch our children into life from the sanctuary of our homes, the intangible gifts of God will go with them and help equip them for his service. In this, the ministry of motherhood will find its completion.

–A MOTHER'S PRAYER–

Dearest Father,
Thank you for choosing to use each of us in the eternal work of your kingdom. Give all of our children a sense of calling on their lives that they might desire to serve you with their whole hearts. Give them boldness and a vision for how you might use their unique personalities and strengths to reach out to others. Help our children in time to become a gift of your grace to their own families and children, passing on your love for generations to come.

Amen

For Study and Discussion

Giving Your Children the Gift of Service

1. Jesus never asks us to do what he has not already been willing to do. John 15:13 states the Lord's definition of the greatest love a person could give. How did he show this kind of love for us? If you strive to follow his example, how would it change the way you parent your children?

2. Name three ways in which you have laid down your own life (goals, time, or expectations) for your children. In what specific areas do your children need to learn how to lay down their own lives and expectations so they can become mature and ready to serve God?

3. In Luke 10:30-37, Jesus tells the parable of the good Samaritan. Read this story to your children. Ask them why this Samaritan, who was not a religious Jew, was considered to be the one who did God's will. What does this teach about how God wants us to act in our daily lives?

4. Try to think of some people you meet every day—in your church, your neighborhood, etc.—who could use some love and care. Come up with a plan to help minister to those people's needs together. (Your children's ideas may surprise and challenge you!)

5. Read Luke 15:1-7. In this passage, what was the attitude of the Pharisee and the scribe about "sinners"? What does Jesus' story indicate about how God feels about "sinners" or "lost sheep"? Make a list of people that your family can pray for and seek to reach out to. Choose one and pray together regularly for this person.

NOTES

Chapter 1: Out of the Boat—a Model for Grace
1. This story is based on John 21.

Chapter 4: The Grace of Forgiveness in Action
1. Oliver Hunkin, *Dangerous Journey: The Story of Pilgrim's Progress,* ill. Alan Parry (Grand Rapids, Mich.: Eerdmans, 1985). This is a children's version of the Christian classic—one of our favorites.

Chapter 5: On the Mountain—a Model for Inspiration
1. This story is based on accounts in Mark 16, Luke 24, and Acts 1. For references to Jesus on Mount Olivet (the Mount of Olives), see John 8:1-11; Matthew 21:1-22; Mark 11:1-11; Luke 21:37; Luke 22:39-48.

Chapter 9: Enough for a Lifetime—a Model for Faith
1. This story is based on tradition and John's description in Revelation 1:9. The words attributed to John here are from 1 John 2:17 and 25. The scenes John remembers are from Matthew 5:11-12; Mark 10:29-30; John 14:3; John 17:24; Matthew 28:19-20; and Acts 1:9-11.

Chapter 13: Persistent Miracles—a Model for Training
1. This account is based on Mark 6:30-55 and 8:1-21.

Chapter 17: Compassionate Harvest—a Model for Service
1. This story is based on accounts in Matthew 8, 9, and 12. The disciples' memory of Jesus in the synagogue comes from Luke 4:16-19.

About Sally Clarkson

Sally Clarkson has been biblically teaching and encouraging others since giving her life to Christ in college. After graduation, she ministered to students and executive women for three years in the states, and for three years in Communist Eastern Europe. After their marriage in 1981, she and Clay served the Lord in overseas missions, and in various churches where Clay was on the pastoral staff. Since 1994, they have both served full time in Whole Heart Ministries, a Christian home and parenting ministry they started by faith to encourage and equip parents to raise wholehearted Christian children. Sally has become a champion of Christian motherhood, speaking to thousands of mothers in dozens of WholeHearted Mother and Mom Heart Conferences since 1998, and writing popular books for Christian mothers, including *The Mission of Motherhood, Seasons of a Mother's Heart,* and *The Mom Walk.* Through a new small groups initiative called Mom Heart Ministry, she seeks to restore mothers' hearts to God's biblical design for motherhood. Discipleship is the heartbeat of her messages, which are filled with personal warmth, biblical insights, and practical help. She also posts regularly on her blog for Christian women at itakejoy.com, and on the momheart.org website. For more information about Sally's speaking ministry, or about Mom Heart Ministry, contact her at:

Whole Heart Ministries
www.wholeheart.org
whm@wholeheart.org
888-488-4HOME (488-4466)